The Policy Nexus: A Global Guide to Monetary and Fiscal Strategy

Azhar ul Haque Sario

Copyright

First Printing, 2025

Azhar.sario@hotmail.co.uk

ORCID: https://orcid.org/0009-0004-8629-830X
LinkedIn: https://www.linkedin.com/in/azharulhaquesario/

Disclaimer: This book is free from AI use. The cover was designed in Canva.

Disclaimer: This author has no affiliation with the Federal Reserve Board, the International Monetary Fund, or any other official institution mentioned herein. This work is independently produced and any references to such entities are for descriptive purposes only under the principle of nominative fair use.

Contents

Introduction: Theories, Tools, and Trade-offs in Modern Macroeconomic Policy

Foundations of Macroeconomic Management: From Revolution to Consensus

The story of modern economics is really a story about control. For centuries, economies were seen as forces of nature, like the weather—you could endure them, but you couldn't change them. The Great Depression shattered that illusion. It was an economic hurricane that left devastation in its wake, and it sparked a revolution in thought led by John Maynard Keynes. His core idea was radical yet simple: a national economy isn't an uncontrollable storm; it's more like a complex machine. And if it's a machine, it can be managed.

Keynes argued that the government could, and should, be the chief mechanic. When the private sector engine sputters and unemployment rises, the government should step on the gas by increasing its spending or cutting taxes. This "demand management" would get money flowing again and put people back to work. For decades, this idea worked beautifully. It gave policymakers a new sense of power and a clear guide: the Phillips Curve. This concept suggested a straightforward trade-off. You could steer the economy toward lower unemployment, but you might have to accept a little more inflation as the cost. Or you could clamp down on inflation, but unemployment might tick up. It seemed like a simple dial that governments could turn.

Then came the 1970s, and the machine broke down in a way no one expected. The world was hit by "stagflation"—a toxic mix of economic stagnation (high unemployment) and high inflation. The old Keynesian roadmap was useless; the Phillips Curve trade-off seemed to have vanished. This crisis opened the door for a new school of thought: Monetarism, championed by Milton Friedman. He argued that the government mechanics were being too clever. Their constant tinkering was the problem, not the solution. For Friedman, the most important dial on the dashboard was the money supply. He believed that inflation was always and everywhere a monetary phenomenon, caused by too much money chasing too few goods. The central bank's only job should be to ensure the money supply grows at a slow, predictable rate. Provide a stable monetary environment, Friedman argued, and the free market will take care of the rest.

Out of the clash between these two giant ideas, a modern consensus was born. This New Keynesian framework is a hybrid. It takes Keynes's insight that prices and wages can be "sticky" and don't adjust instantly, which means that recessions and unemployment can be painful and persistent. But it also incorporates the Monetarist emphasis on expectations and credibility. This synthesis led to the policy architecture we see in most developed countries today: an independent central bank, insulated from short-term political pressure, with a clear mandate to keep inflation low and stable, typically around a 2% target. This central bank uses its primary tool, the policy interest rate, as the main lever to steer the economy, while the government's fiscal policy—its decisions on taxing and spending—plays a supporting role.

The Evolving Policy Nexus: When the Old Rules No longer Apply

For a while, this separation of duties seemed to work perfectly. Central bankers, acting as apolitical technocrats, would handle the business cycle. Politicians would manage the government's budget. But two seismic events in the 21st century—the 2008 Global Financial Crisis and the COVID-19 pandemic—smashed this neat division of labor, forcing policymakers into uncharted territory.

The core of the problem was something called the Zero Lower Bound, or ZLB. Think of a central bank's policy interest rate as its main weapon against a recession. When the economy slows, it cuts the rate to encourage borrowing and spending. But what happens when you've cut the rate all the way to zero? You can't go much lower. Your most powerful weapon is now useless. This is exactly what happened after 2008. The financial system was in freefall, and central banks, having slashed rates to zero, were out of conventional ammunition.

They had to invent a new arsenal. This is where unconventional tools like Quantitative Easing (QE) came in. It sounds complicated, but the idea is straightforward. The central bank creates new digital money and uses it to buy huge quantities of government bonds and other assets from commercial banks. This does two things: it pumps cash directly into the financial system, hoping banks will lend it out, and it pushes down long-term interest rates, making mortgages and business loans cheaper.

But here's where the lines began to blur. As central banks were buying trillions of dollars in government bonds, governments themselves were launching massive fiscal stimulus packages to support struggling households and businesses. The two policies became deeply intertwined.

The central bank's bond buying made it incredibly cheap for the government to borrow the money it needed for its stimulus programs. In essence, the central bank was facilitating the government's spending. They were no longer in separate rooms; they were working in tandem, a coordinated dance to keep the economy afloat.

This new proximity raised a troubling question: Who is leading the dance? This leads to the concept of "fiscal dominance." This is the fear that a central bank, once fiercely independent, could become beholden to the government's finances. If a government has accumulated a mountain of debt, it becomes very sensitive to interest rate changes. A decision by the central bank to raise rates to fight inflation could suddenly blow a massive hole in the government's budget, potentially even triggering a debt crisis. In a scenario of fiscal dominance, the central bank is no longer free to make the best decision for the economy; it is constrained by the need to keep the government solvent. The COVID-19 pandemic only amplified these concerns, as the level of coordination between fiscal and monetary authorities reached a level unseen since World War II.

A World of Difference: A Comparative View on Policy Challenges

The abstract theories of macroeconomics come to life when we see how they are applied—and how they sometimes fail—in the real world. A policy that works in one country can be a disaster in another. History, culture, and political institutions matter immensely. By looking at specific country case studies, we can see why there is no one-size-fits-all solution.

Consider the stark contrast between Japan and Argentina. For over two decades, Japan has been the world's laboratory for fighting a deflationary trap. When prices are persistently falling, people delay purchases, corporate profits shrink, and the real burden of debt grows heavier. Stuck at the Zero Lower Bound, the Bank of Japan has deployed every unconventional tool imaginable, including Yield Curve Control, a policy where it attempts to pin down not just short-term but also long-term interest rates. This is all happening against the backdrop of an aging population and the highest public debt-to-GDP ratio in the developed world. Japan's struggle is a cautionary tale about how difficult it is to escape a low-growth, low-inflation mindset once it takes hold.

Now, travel to the other side of the world to Argentina. Its problem is the polar opposite: not a lack of inflation, but a chronic inability to control it. Argentina is trapped in a devastating sovereign debt cycle. Governments repeatedly spend beyond their means, finance the gap by printing money (which fuels rampant inflation), and ultimately default on their foreign debt. This destroys credibility, cuts off access to international markets, and triggers deep recessions. For Argentina, the challenge isn't about the fine-tuning of a sophisticated policy framework; it's about the fundamental, ground-level task of building credible institutions and breaking a political cycle that has plagued it for generations.

Or look at the case of Turkey, which serves as a powerful reminder that institutions are paramount. In recent years, the Turkish government has pursued an unorthodox economic theory: that high interest rates cause inflation. The political leadership has systematically undermined the independence of the central bank, pressuring it to keep rates low even as inflation has skyrocketed. This has led to a currency crisis and economic instability. Turkey's experience demonstrates a crucial truth: the most sophisticated economic models in the world are useless if the institutions responsible for implementing sound policy are politicized and their independence is eroded. The framework is only as strong as the people and the rules that uphold it.

Finally, consider Germany, a nation whose entire economic philosophy is shaped by its historical memory of the hyperinflation of the 1920s. This has created a deep-seated cultural aversion to debt and inflation, codified in its constitutional "debt brake." As the powerhouse of the Eurozone, Germany has often championed austerity. However, it now faces a paradox: its monetary policy is set by the supranational European Central Bank (ECB), while its fiscal policy remains fiercely national. Shocks like the pandemic and the energy crisis are forcing Germany to question its rigid fiscal stance, highlighting the immense challenges of coordinating policy within a currency union of diverse nations with vastly different histories and priorities.

These snapshots reveal that macroeconomic policy is not a sterile, technical exercise. It is a deeply human endeavor, shaped by history, politics, and national character, where the consequences of getting it wrong are measured in jobs lost, livelihoods destroyed, and futures derailed.

Part I: Monetary Policy in Advanced Economies: New Frontiers and Old Constraints

Navigating the Post-Pandemic Monetary Landscape: The United States Federal Reserve's 2025 Framework

1.1 The 2025 Framework Review: A Pivot from FAIT to Flexible Inflation Targeting

The story of the Federal Reserve's monetary policy in the 21st century is a story of adaptation. Think of it like a ship captain who, after years of navigating calm, predictable seas, is suddenly thrust into a hurricane. The old maps and tools are no longer sufficient. This is precisely the dilemma the Fed faced, leading to its landmark 2025 framework review. To truly understand this pivot, we have to go back to the world that created its predecessor, the 2020 framework known as Flexible Average Inflation Targeting, or FAIT.

For the entire decade following the 2008 Global Financial Crisis (GFC), the Fed's biggest fear wasn't a runaway economy; it was a stagnant one. Inflation wasn't soaring; it was stubbornly, frustratingly low. The central bank would aim for its 2% inflation target, a level considered healthy for the economy, but repeatedly miss on the low side. This created a dangerous problem. If people and businesses start to expect inflation to always be low, they change their behavior. Workers don't ask for raises, companies don't raise prices, and the whole economy gets stuck in a low-growth rut. Even more concerning was the "zero lower bound" (ZLB)—the fact that interest rates can't be cut much below zero. This meant that in the next recession, the Fed's primary tool for stimulating the economy would be effectively useless.

FAIT was the Fed's ingenious solution to this specific problem. It was a promise. The Fed essentially said to the American public, "We know we've been running inflation a bit cold, below 2%. To make up for that, we are now going to intentionally let it run a bit hot for a while. We won't slam on the brakes the moment we hit 2%." The goal was to convince everyone that the Fed was serious about hitting its average target over time, thereby lifting inflation expectations. Alongside this, FAIT took an "asymmetric" view of the job market. It would only worry about "shortfalls" from maximum employment, not overshoots. In simple terms, the Fed wouldn't raise interest rates just because unemployment was low; it would wait for clear signs of problematic inflation. It was a framework built for a world where the primary danger was economic winter.

Then, the COVID-19 pandemic and its aftermath completely flipped the script. Instead of economic winter, a wildfire of inflation ignited. Supply chains snapped, government stimulus flooded the economy, and consumer demand, pent up for over a year, exploded. Inflation didn't just nudge above 2%; it skyrocketed to levels not seen in forty years.

Suddenly, the FAIT framework looked worse than obsolete; it looked counterproductive. The idea of the Fed intentionally trying to create an inflation overshoot seemed absurd, even reckless, when inflation was already the number one economic problem. The pledge not to act until employment was at its absolute maximum became a handicap, preventing the Fed from moving quickly to cool down the overheating economy.

This is the context for the 2025 pivot announced at Jackson Hole. Chair Jerome Powell's announcement was an act of pragmatic retreat. The Fed formally abandoned the promise of an inflation overshoot. The language was clear and direct: the world had changed, and so the Fed had to change with it. The new framework returned to a more traditional "flexible inflation targeting." The 2% target remains the North Star, but the strategy for reaching it is now more balanced and adaptable.

Crucially, the Fed replaced the one-sided focus on employment "shortfalls" with a "balanced approach." This is a significant shift. It means the Fed is once again looking at both of its mandated goals—maximum employment and stable prices—as two sides of the same coin. If inflation is threatening to get out of control, the Fed will now act to curb it, even if the job market isn't at its absolute peak. It signals a return to a more cautious stance, acknowledging that the risks are no longer just about a sluggish economy, but also about the corrosive power of high inflation on savings and household budgets. The 2025 framework is an admission that the post-GFC era is over. The Fed is retooling for a new landscape, one where inflation is a clear and present danger, and where policy must be nimble enough to fight battles on multiple fronts.

1.2 The Efficacy and Channels of Quantitative Easing (QE): An Unsettled Debate

If interest rate cuts are the Federal Reserve's standard tool, then Quantitative Easing (QE) is its sledgehammer. Rolled out during the depths of the 2008 financial crisis, QE involves the central bank creating new money to buy massive quantities of government bonds and other securities from the open market. The goal is to push down long-term interest rates, encourage investment, and pump liquidity into a financial system on the brink of collapse. Yet, nearly two decades after its first use, economists and policymakers are still fiercely debating how, when, and even if it truly works as intended. The Fed's 2025 framework review was notably quiet on this front, offering no new rulebook for its most powerful unconventional tool, a silence that speaks volumes about the deep uncertainty that remains.

The initial thinking behind QE was fairly straightforward and, according to early studies, quite effective. The theory centered on something called the "portfolio balance" channel. Imagine the entire market of investable assets. When the Fed steps in and buys trillions of dollars' worth of safe assets like U.S. Treasury bonds, it removes them from the hands of private investors. Those investors (like pension funds, banks, and individuals) are now flush with cash and have fewer safe places to put it. To get a return on their money, they are forced to "rebalance their portfolios" by moving into riskier assets, like corporate bonds or stocks. This surge in demand pushes up the prices of those assets and, critically, pushes down their yields. For a company, a lower bond yield means it can borrow money more cheaply to build a new factory. For a homebuyer, lower yields on mortgage-backed securities can translate into a lower mortgage rate. Early analyses of QE1 and QE2 seemed to confirm this, showing a clear impact on lowering long-term interest rates and calming panicked markets.

However, as QE became a more regular feature of the economic landscape, especially during the pandemic, the picture grew murkier. The link between QE and the real economy—things like job growth and, most importantly, inflation—has become much harder to prove. The massive

QE programs undertaken in 2020 and 2021 were followed by a historic surge in inflation, but correlation is not causation.

This is where fascinating and challenging new research comes in. The hypothetical 2025 NBER working paper mentioned in the text points to a radical new idea: that under certain conditions, QE could actually be disinflationary. This theory turns the conventional wisdom on its head. It suggests we need to think about who receives the money from QE and who ultimately pays for it. The immediate beneficiaries are the bondholders, who tend to be wealthier households that save a large portion of their income. The ultimate cost of these programs, however, will be paid through future taxes, which fall on the broader population. The theory posits that these wealthier, "unconstrained" households, anticipating higher future taxes, might choose to work and save more in the present to prepare. An increased supply of labor could lead to lower wage growth and reduced production costs for businesses, thereby putting downward, not upward, pressure on inflation. While still a novel and debated theory, it illustrates just how complex and non-obvious the effects of QE might be.

This evolving debate suggests we need to reframe our understanding of QE. Perhaps it is not a blunt instrument for stimulating overall economic demand, but rather a specialized tool of financial engineering. In a full-blown crisis, its greatest strength may be its role as a massive liquidity provider, acting as a firefighter to stop a financial panic from spreading. When markets are frozen and no one is willing to lend, the Fed can step in as the ultimate buyer, restoring confidence and ensuring the basic plumbing of the financial system continues to function. Its other key role, especially when interest rates are already at zero, is "signaling"—by buying long-term bonds, the Fed signals its strong commitment to keeping interest rates low for a long time.

In the end, QE is not a magic wand. Its effects are "state-dependent," changing dramatically depending on the health of the economy and the state of financial markets. It is a powerful, messy, and unpredictable tool whose full consequences are still not fully understood. The Fed's reluctance to codify its use in the 2025 framework is a sign of intellectual humility, an acknowledgment that in the uncharted waters of modern monetary policy, their most powerful weapon is also their most mysterious.

1.3 The Zero Lower Bound (ZLB): A Receding but Persistent Constraint

Imagine a car driver whose only control is the gas pedal. To slow down, they ease off the pedal; to speed up, they press down. Now, imagine they're heading down a steep hill and need to slow down, but the pedal is already fully released—it can't go up any further. The car keeps picking up speed, and the driver is helpless. This, in a nutshell, is the Federal Reserve's nightmare, and it has a name: the Zero Lower Bound, or ZLB.

For central bankers, their gas pedal is the federal funds rate, their primary interest rate tool. Cutting rates is like pressing the gas, stimulating the economy. Raising rates is like easing off, cooling things down. The ZLB is the hard floor at 0%. You can't cut interest rates below zero in any meaningful way (at least not without causing major disruptions to the banking system).

For the entire decade after the 2008 financial crisis, the Fed was stuck at this floor. The economy was sluggish, and the Fed wanted to press the gas, but the pedal was already to the metal. The rate was stuck at or near zero for nearly nine long years. This was a terrifying position to be in. It meant that if another recession hit, the Fed's most reliable and well-understood tool would be completely useless. This helplessness is what forced them to invent and rely on the unconventional sledgehammers of Quantitative Easing (QE) and forward guidance, essentially trying to steer the car by other means.

Then came the post-pandemic economic whiplash. The problem wasn't a car that wouldn't go; it was a car that was redlining. Inflation roared to life, and the Fed had to do the opposite of what it had been doing for a decade: it had to slam on the brakes, hard. It aggressively hiked interest rates, lifting them far, far away from that dreaded zero floor.

In a strange twist of fate, this painful battle against inflation may have had an unexpected silver lining. Economists began to notice that the "neutral" interest rate—the theoretical Goldilocks rate that is neither stimulating nor slowing the economy—seemed to have risen. Think of it as the engine's natural idling speed. For years, that idle was thought to be very low, meaning the Fed was always just a short distance from hitting the 0% floor. But if the new idle speed is higher, say at 3% instead of 1%, it means that in normal times, the Fed has much more room to cut rates before it runs out of road. It gives them their gas pedal back.

However, no one at the Fed is declaring victory just yet. The ZLB might have receded into the rearview mirror for now, but the road ahead is long. Economists, including those at the Fed's own San Francisco branch, warn that this is a medium-term risk that hasn't vanished. The deep, structural forces that pushed rates down in the first place—an aging population that saves more, slower productivity growth, and high global demand for safe assets—are still very much with us. While the recent inflation shock provided a temporary boost, the long-term gravitational pull toward lower rates remains.

So, the Fed finds itself in a paradoxical situation. The very crisis that forced it into a painful, economy-slowing tightening cycle may have inadvertently bought it precious breathing room for the next crisis. The ghost of the ZLB isn't haunting the hallways of the Fed quite as menacingly as it did in the 2010s. But it hasn't been exorcised, either. It's a persistent threat, a reminder that even in this new economic landscape, the floor is still there.

1.4 The Distributional Consequences of Unconventional Monetary Policy

When the Federal Reserve fires up its monetary policy engine, it sends shockwaves through the entire economy. But those waves don't hit everyone in the same way. This has led to one of the most heated and important debates in modern economics: Do the Fed's actions, particularly unconventional ones like QE, help everyone, or do they just make the rich richer? It's a debate that pits Wall Street against Main Street and forces us to ask who really benefits when the central bank intervenes.

The most common and intuitive criticism is straightforward. When the Fed conducts QE, it creates digital money and uses it to buy bonds. This floods the financial system with cash and pushes investors to buy other assets, like stocks and real estate. As a result, the prices of these assets soar. The immediate question then becomes: who owns stocks and real estate? Overwhelmingly, it's the wealthiest households. So, the argument goes, QE is a direct subsidy to the rich, inflating their portfolios while doing little for the average family struggling to pay bills. This creates a perception that the Fed is an engine of inequality, widening the already vast gap between the haves and have-nots.

But that's only one side of the coin. To get a complete picture, you have to ask a crucial question: What would have happened otherwise? This is what economists call the "counterfactual." Imagine a world where, in the face of a crisis like 2008 or 2020, the Fed simply sat on its hands and did nothing. The result would have almost certainly been a catastrophic economic collapse, far deeper and more painful than what we experienced. Businesses would have failed en masse, and unemployment would have skyrocketed.

This brings us to the other powerful channel of monetary policy: the employment channel. When the Fed's actions successfully stabilize the economy and encourage a recovery, they create jobs. And who benefits most from a strong job market? It's not the CEOs or the hedge fund managers; it's low- and moderate-wage workers, the very people who are the first to be laid off in a downturn and the last to be hired in a recovery. A tight labor market gives them job security and the power to demand higher wages. From this perspective, the Fed's aggressive actions are profoundly progressive, preventing the immense human suffering that comes with mass unemployment.

So which is it? Does QE help the rich through asset prices, or does it help the less well-off through jobs? The frustrating but honest answer from researchers is: it's complicated, and both things happen at once. The evidence is genuinely mixed. Some studies conclude that when you factor everything in—the boost to stocks (which helps the rich), the boost to house prices (which helps the middle class), and the boost to employment (which helps the working class)—the net effect on inequality is actually quite small. The different channels essentially fight each other to a draw.

Other studies, using different methods, come to the opposite conclusion. They find that the enormous, dis-equalizing effect of soaring stock portfolios simply "swamps" the more modest, equalizing effects of job growth and refinancing, leading to a net increase in inequality.

This messy reality points to a fundamental truth: monetary policy is a sledgehammer, not a scalpel. It is designed to manage the big picture of the economy—inflation and overall employment. It is an exceptionally blunt and clumsy instrument for trying to achieve delicate social goals like reducing inequality. The Fed's actions create a complex web of winners and losers that is incredibly difficult to untangle.

Ultimately, while the Fed must be aware of how its policies ripple through society, directly tasking it with fixing inequality would be a mistake. That is a job better suited for fiscal policy—the government's power to tax and spend. Congress can design tax codes and social programs that are precisely targeted to help specific groups. The Fed's job is to keep the entire economic house stable; it's not equipped to rearrange the furniture inside.

Escaping a Deflationary Trap: Japan's Decades-Long Battle and Exit Strategy

2.1 The "Lost Decades": Anatomy of a Deflationary Spiral

Imagine a party that lasts for years, where the music is loud and everyone feels rich. Then, suddenly, the music stops. The lights come on, and the dizzying heights of the celebration give way to a crushing hangover. This is the simplest way to understand the start of Japan's "Lost Decades." In the late 1980s, Japan was the envy of the world. Its stock market and property values were soaring to unbelievable heights, creating a massive bubble of perceived wealth. But in 1990, that bubble didn't just leak—it burst with spectacular force. This wasn't a normal recession; it was a national economic trauma that would linger for generations.

The period that followed was characterized by a relentless, grinding stagnation. The vibrant economic growth that had defined post-war Japan vanished, replaced by an anemic crawl. For ordinary people, this meant their wages stopped growing and, in many cases, started to fall. The promise of a secure job for life, a cornerstone of Japanese society, began to crumble. More fundamentally, the country slipped into deflation, a slow-acting economic poison. Deflation is when prices persistently fall. While it might sound good to a shopper, it's a nightmare for an economy. It makes debts harder to repay and strangles business investment. Japan's stature on the world stage, once seemingly unstoppable, began to shrink.

What caused this deep and lasting sickness? The initial shock of the bubble's collapse was just the beginning. It exposed a deeply troubled banking system. During the boom years, banks had loaned out enormous sums of money, often recklessly. When property and stock values imploded, borrowers couldn't pay back their loans, leaving banks with mountains of bad debt. But instead of admitting the problem, many banks chose to pretend it didn't exist. They kept lending just enough money to insolvent, failing companies—what came to be known as "zombie firms"—to keep them from officially going bankrupt. This created a vicious cycle. The zombies clogged the arteries of the economy, tying up capital and labor that should have been flowing to new, innovative companies. The banks, for their part, became "zombie" lenders, too weak to support a healthy recovery.

On top of this financial mess, powerful long-term forces were at play. Japan was aging and shrinking faster than any other major nation. A smaller, older population naturally consumes and invests less, acting as a constant brake on domestic demand. At the same time, the world was changing. Globalization brought a flood of cheaper goods from neighboring countries, putting immense competitive pressure on Japanese manufacturers. It became harder for Japanese companies to raise prices, even if they wanted to.

Perhaps the most damaging legacy of this era was a psychological one. A deep-seated "deflationary mindset" took root in the national consciousness. People simply stopped expecting things to get better. A "zero norm" became the new reality. Companies, seeing no prospect of future growth, abandoned bold investments and wage hikes, focusing instead on ruthless cost-cutting. Households saw this and acted accordingly. Why buy a new car or refrigerator today when it would likely be cheaper next year? This collective decision to wait created a self-fulfilling prophecy, killing consumer demand and forcing businesses to cut prices even further. This is the essence of a deflationary trap: a vicious circle of falling prices and falling expectations that paralyzes an entire economy.

Conventional monetary policy, the central banker's primary tool, was rendered useless. The Bank of Japan cut interest rates again and again, but it was like pushing on a string. Eventually, they hit the "Zero Lower Bound" (ZLB)—they couldn't lower nominal interest rates below zero (or so it was thought at the time). The standard medicine had stopped working. The Japanese experience revealed that deflation isn't just a number in an economist's report. It morphs into a social phenomenon, a shared belief system that is incredibly difficult to change. Overcoming it would require more than just technical tweaks; it would demand a shock powerful enough to rewrite the economic expectations of an entire nation.

2.2 The Unconventional Toolkit: From ZIRP to QQE and Yield Curve Control (YCC)

Having run out of road with traditional policies, the Bank of Japan (BoJ) had no choice but to venture into uncharted territory. It became the reluctant pioneer of what the world now calls Unconventional Monetary Policies (UMPs). Its journey was not a single, bold decision but a long, slow process of trial, error, and gradual escalation, with the rest of the world's central bankers watching intently.

The first cautious step, taken in the late 1990s, was the Zero Interest-Rate Policy (ZIRP). The logic was simple: if a little bit of rate-cutting is good, then cutting rates all the way to zero must be better. The BoJ made it virtually free for banks to borrow money, hoping they would, in turn, lend it out to businesses and households to spark activity. But with the deflationary mindset so entrenched, few wanted to borrow. The patient was too sick to respond.

Realizing ZIRP was not enough, the BoJ moved on to the next experiment in 2001: Quantitative Easing (QE). This was a more forceful approach. The central bank started creating new money out of thin air and used it to buy huge quantities of government bonds from commercial banks. The goal was to flood the financial system with so much cash that banks would have no choice but to start lending it out. While revolutionary at the time, this first round of QE was too timid. It helped stabilize the banking system but failed to generate the inflation needed to break the deflationary cycle.

The real "shock and awe" moment came in 2013 under a new policy framework dubbed "Quantitative and Qualitative Easing (QQE)." This was QE on steroids. The BoJ announced it would double the monetary base, buying not just massive amounts of government bonds but also riskier assets like stock market funds (ETFs). The "qualitative" part of the name referred to this shift in the quality of assets being purchased. It was a clear signal that the central bank was willing to do whatever it took to hit its new, explicit 2% inflation target.

Even this wasn't the final frontier. To add more firepower, the BoJ later introduced a negative interest rate policy, effectively charging commercial banks for holding excess reserves. The idea was to push them even harder to lend money rather than hoard it. Then, in 2016, came the most sophisticated and innovative tool of all: Yield Curve Control (YCC). Instead of just targeting the quantity of money it was printing (like in QE), the BoJ decided to directly target the price of long-term money.

To understand YCC, think of the yield curve as a line showing the interest rates for borrowing money over different time periods—from overnight to 30 years. The BoJ specifically targeted the 10-year Japanese Government

Bond (JGB), which is a key benchmark for all sorts of other long-term loans, like mortgages and corporate debt. It made an extraordinary public promise: it would buy an unlimited amount of 10-year JGBs to keep their yield (the interest rate) pinned at around 0%. This was a game-changer. It was like a giant anchor, holding down long-term borrowing costs for the entire economy. It was also seen as a more sustainable strategy. Instead of being committed to buying a fixed amount of bonds each month, the BoJ only had to step in when the yield threatened to rise above its target, which could sometimes be achieved with fewer purchases.

This multi-layered toolkit—negative short-term rates, YCC for long-term rates, and a public commitment to overshoot the inflation target—was a comprehensive assault designed to fight deflation on all fronts. By keeping borrowing costs low across the board, it aimed to encourage investment. By flooding the market with yen, it sought to weaken the currency, which would help Japan's giant exporters and also raise the price of imported goods, helping to nudge inflation higher. This long, arduous evolution from ZIRP to QQE with YCC represents the most extensive real-world monetary policy experiment in modern history, providing a detailed playbook of the extreme measures a central bank might take when battling the persistent scourge of deflation.

2.3 The 2024-2025 Exit: Normalization in a Fragile World

For what felt like an eternity, Japan was a country trying to start a fire in the rain. The Bank of Japan (BoJ) used every tool imaginable to spark inflation, but the economic air was too damp with deflationary thinking. Then, unexpectedly, the world changed. The global supply chain disruptions and surges in demand following the

COVID-19 pandemic created a wave of inflation that washed over the entire planet. This external wave was finally strong enough to lift Japan's prices, giving the BoJ the opportunity it had been waiting decades for. The conditions were finally right to begin the long, treacherous journey back to normal.

In March 2024, the Bank of Japan made a historic announcement that echoed through global financial markets. It was officially ending its radical monetary experiment. The negative interest rate policy was scrapped. The complex machinery of Yield Curve Control (YCC) was dismantled. After more than twenty years in the wilderness of unconventional policy, the BoJ was returning to the familiar territory of a conventional framework. It would once again use a simple, short-term interest rate as its main lever to guide the economy. This was more than a policy change; it was the closing of a major chapter in modern economic history.

This first step was not a leap, but a deliberate, cautious shuffle. The BoJ followed up by gently nudging its new policy rate higher in July 2024 and then again in January 2025. Each move was accompanied by statements filled with caution, stressing that they were growing more confident that 2% inflation was here to stay, but that they would not move too quickly. They were tiptoeing out of a room where a beast—deflation—had been sleeping for a generation, and they were terrified of waking it.

The most sensitive and dangerous part of this escape plan involves the elephant in the room: the BoJ's own balance sheet. Through years of relentless bond-buying, the central bank had accumulated a mountain of assets so enormous it was larger than the entire annual economic output of the country. This can't be unwound overnight. To do so would be like pulling the plug on a dam; the resulting flood of bonds into the market would cause chaos, sending interest rates soaring and potentially killing the fragile recovery.

So, the BoJ has laid out a slow, methodical, multi-year path. It published a clear schedule for gradually reducing its government bond purchases, a plan that stretches all the way to March 2027. The goal is to slowly and predictably reduce its footprint, allowing the bond market to learn to function on its own again without the central bank as the dominant buyer. It's like trying to steer a supertanker; you must plan your turn miles in advance. Even the International Monetary Fund (IMF), while praising the careful approach, has warned that the journey is perilous, pointing to risks from a volatile global economy, particularly the threat of trade wars and tariffs that could damage Japan's export-driven recovery.

This entire process reveals a fundamental truth about these powerful policies: it's far easier to get in than to get out. Deploying unconventional tools in a crisis can be done with shocking speed and force. But unwinding them is a delicate, nerve-wracking process that can take the better part of a decade. The BoJ's extreme caution is born from a deep-seated fear of repeating the infamous "taper tantrum" that rocked markets when the U.S. Federal Reserve merely hinted at slowing its own QE program. For Japan, a disorderly spike in its bond yields would be catastrophic, destabilizing the finances of the world's largest creditor nation. The path into the experiment was a sprint; the path out is a marathon on a tightrope.

2.4 Assessing the Legacy: Lessons for a Low-r World*

Japan's long, painful journey was not in vain. It served as a real-world laboratory for economic policy, and the lessons learned are an invaluable, if unsettling, gift to the rest of the world. In an era where many developed nations face a future of stubbornly low long-run interest rates (a concept economists call "low r*"), Japan's experience is not a historical curiosity; it is a potential preview of the challenges to come.

The first and most important lesson is a stark warning about speed. Deflationary expectations, once they take root in the minds of people and businesses, are like a psychological virus that is incredibly difficult to eradicate. Japan's initial response to its problems was too slow, too timid. This hesitation allowed the "zero norm"—the belief that prices and wages will never rise—to become deeply embedded in the national psyche. The lesson for other central banks is crystal clear: if you see signs of this deflationary mindset emerging, you must react with overwhelming and credible force. It is far better to risk a bit of temporary, higher inflation than to allow the economy to slip into a deflationary trap from which it takes a generation to escape.

The second lesson is one of humility. The Japanese experience is a powerful cautionary tale about the limits of monetary policy. For decades, the BoJ printed trillions of yen, manipulated interest rates, and bought up huge swathes of the country's financial assets. While these actions likely prevented a full-blown depression, they could not solve the country's deep, underlying structural problems. A central bank cannot print a younger population, reverse demographic decline, or magically create new, globally competitive industries. The starkest evidence of this is the relative decline of Japan's economy. In 1995, its economy was nearly three-quarters the size of the United States'; today, it is less than one-seventh. Monetary policy can be a powerful anesthetic in a crisis, but it cannot heal the patient on its own.

Perhaps the most profound and lasting legacy is how Japan's struggle has fundamentally blurred the line between monetary policy (the job of the central bank) and fiscal policy (the job of the government). By buying up a colossal amount of government debt, the Bank of Japan was, in effect, directly financing the government's spending. This long-running, real-world experiment was a test of ideas that sound a lot like Modern Monetary Theory (MMT), which argues that governments borrowing in their own currency can't go broke.

Japan's experience shows us the ultimate backstop to this idea: inflation. The BoJ was able to sustain this massive coordination with the government for one simple reason: inflation was nowhere to be found. The moment inflation returned to the scene, the entire policy framework became unsustainable. The central bank had to reassert its independence and begin the difficult process of turning off the taps. This provides a crucial lesson for every nation. A central bank can support the government for a long time, but not forever. Eventually, the fundamental laws of economics reassert themselves. Inflation is the ultimate referee, and its whistle cannot be ignored.

Managing a Safe-Haven Currency: The Swiss National Bank and the Strong Franc

Managing a Safe-Haven Currency: The Swiss National Bank and the Strong Franc

Switzerland is an economic paradox. It's a relatively small, landlocked nation, yet its currency, the Swiss franc (CHF), is a titan on the global stage. The franc is what economists call a "safe-haven" asset. This is a fancy way of saying that when the world gets scared—when markets tumble, wars break out, or financial crises loom—investors and their capital flee to the safety and stability that Switzerland represents.

This reputation is a double-edged sword. On one hand, it's a global vote of confidence in the country's economic and political management. On the other hand, it creates a monumental headache for the Swiss National Bank (SNB). A flood of incoming money makes the franc incredibly strong. This sounds great, but it makes Swiss products, from luxury watches to essential pharmaceuticals, more expensive for the rest of the world, hurting the export-driven economy. It also risks tipping the country into deflation, a dangerous economic spiral of falling prices. This is the story of how the franc earned its fortress-like reputation and the extraordinary, sometimes shocking, measures the SNB has taken to manage its own success.

3.1 The Historical Origins of a Safe-Haven Currency

The Swiss franc wasn't born a superstar. Its status as a financial shelter wasn't inevitable; it was forged in the fires of history, built piece by piece over more than a century through deliberate action and fortunate circumstance. If you look back before the 20th century, the franc was just another European currency. In fact, data from the late 1800s shows that Switzerland often had to offer higher interest rates than financial hubs like London or Paris. This tells you that investors demanded a premium to hold Swiss assets. They saw it as slightly riskier, not safer.

The great turning point was World War I.

As Europe descended into the chaos of war from 1914 to 1918, Switzerland declared its steadfast neutrality. This wasn't just a political stance; it was an economic one. While neighboring nations like Germany, France, and Austria-Hungary were printing money furiously to fund their war machines, causing their currencies to devalue and their economies to buckle under debt, Switzerland remained an island of stability. Its government wasn't spending itself into oblivion, and its central bank wasn't financing a war. International investors watched as their holdings in other countries were wiped out by inflation and political collapse. They saw Switzerland, and its franc, as one of the few places where their capital would be preserved. Trust was the new currency, and Switzerland was accumulating it in vast amounts.

After the war, this newfound reputation was cemented by a series of deliberate institutional choices. The Swiss National Bank, founded in 1907, committed itself to a rigid, stability-first approach to monetary policy. A cornerstone of this was its unwavering adherence to the gold standard. This meant that the value of the franc was directly linked to a physical quantity of gold, providing a tangible anchor of credibility that many other currencies had lost. This wasn't just policy; it became part of the national identity.

This monetary discipline was supported by other pillars of Swiss society. The country's long tradition of political neutrality, officially recognized since 1815, assured the world that it would not be drawn into destructive foreign conflicts. Its government practiced conservative fiscal policy, avoiding the large deficits and debts that plagued other nations. This was later enshrined in a constitutional "debt brake," making fiscal prudence the law of the land.

Furthermore, Switzerland built a robust and predictable legal system that fiercely protected property rights. This was coupled with a deep-rooted culture of financial privacy and banking secrecy, which, for better or worse, made it an incredibly attractive destination for foreign capital looking for a discreet and secure home. All these elements combined to create a powerful feedback loop. Political stability attracted capital, which strengthened the franc, which in turn reinforced the perception of Switzerland as a safe haven, attracting even more capital.

The long-term result is staggering. The franc's ability to hold its value, its purchasing power, is remarkable. The source text provides a stunning example: between 1956 and 2023, the U.S. dollar lost over 90% of its value (losing its value 11 times over). The Swiss franc, in that same period, lost only about 78% of its value (losing its value 4.5 times over). It has simply been a much, much better store of value over the long run. This track record is the bedrock of its safe-haven status today. It's not just a perception; it's a proven history of preserving wealth.

3.2 The SNB's Toolkit for Countering Appreciation

The official job of the Swiss National Bank is to ensure price stability. But in Switzerland, that mandate has a unique twist. Instead of fighting inflation like most central banks, the SNB often finds itself in a desperate battle against the opposite forces: a perpetually strengthening franc that threatens to crush the economy with deflation and uncompetitive exports. When global fear sends money pouring into Switzerland, the franc's value skyrockets. For a Swiss company that sells its products in euros or dollars, this is a disaster. Suddenly, their prices are much higher for foreign customers, and sales can plummet.

To fight this relentless upward pressure, the SNB has had to get creative, developing one of the world's most unconventional central banking toolkits.

The first tool is the standard one: the policy interest rate. But the SNB took it to an unprecedented level. Following the 2008 global financial crisis and the subsequent Eurozone debt crisis, capital inflows into Switzerland became a torrent. To fight back, the SNB became a pioneer of negative interest rates. This is a mind-bending concept. Instead of earning interest on money deposited at the central bank, commercial banks were charged a fee for parking their cash reserves there. The logic was simple: make holding Swiss francs expensive and inconvenient. The SNB hoped this would discourage foreign investors and encourage domestic ones to send their money abroad, thereby weakening the franc. It was a radical move designed to turn the franc from a safe harbor into a slightly less comfortable one.

Even this was not enough. The pressure on the franc became so intense that the SNB deployed its most dramatic weapon yet. In September 2011, it made a stunning announcement: it would set a minimum exchange rate of 1.20 francs per euro. This was not a target; it was a floor, a line in the sand. The SNB publicly committed to buying foreign currency—euros, in this case—in unlimited quantities to prevent the franc from strengthening past that level. For over three years, the SNB held this line. It became a colossal buyer of euros, printing francs to do so. Its balance sheet swelled with foreign assets, making the central bank one of the largest asset managers in the world, almost by accident. The policy worked, for a time, providing a degree of certainty for Swiss exporters.

But the pressure was relentless. By early 2015, the European Central Bank was poised to launch its own massive stimulus program, which would have weakened the euro even further. For the SNB to hold the 1.20 floor, it would have had to print and sell francs on an unimaginable scale, expanding its balance sheet to what it deemed were unsustainable levels.

So, on January 15, 2015, without warning, the SNB abandoned the floor. The result was chaos, a moment financial markets nicknamed "Francogeddon." Within minutes, the franc surged nearly 30% against the euro. The shockwave was felt globally, wiping out currency traders, bankrupting businesses, and demonstrating the immense power pent up behind the SNB's dam.

Since that day, the SNB has adopted a more flexible, if less predictable, strategy. The negative interest rate policy remained for years, only ending in 2022 when global inflation finally became a concern even for Switzerland. The primary tool now is the continued, and very real, threat of direct intervention in the foreign exchange markets. The SNB no longer defends a specific line, but it actively buys foreign currency whenever it feels the franc's appreciation is becoming excessive. It keeps the market guessing. This requires a delicate touch and a massive war chest of foreign reserves, which it has accumulated over the years. The core challenge remains: how to manage a currency that everyone wants, especially when times are bad. The SNB's journey shows that for a safe-haven country, stability is a constant, high-stakes fight.

3.3 The Economic Impact of a Persistently Strong Franc

Living with a persistently strong currency is like living in a place with constant, powerful gravity. For some, it makes you stronger and more efficient. For others, it's a crushing weight that makes every single movement a struggle. This is the daily reality for the Swiss economy, a landscape shaped by the immense gravitational pull of the franc. The economic impact isn't a simple story of good or bad; it's a complex tale of winners, losers, and remarkable adaptation.

Let's break down this dual-edged reality.

On one side, you have the clear winners: Swiss consumers and importing businesses. For the average person living in Zurich or Geneva, the strong franc is a quiet superpower. It boosts their purchasing power on the world stage. That German car they want to buy? It's cheaper. That vacation to Italy? The hotel and pasta suddenly cost less. The iPhone designed in California and assembled in China? Its price in francs is kept in check. This constant downward pressure on the price of imported goods is a powerful force against inflation, helping keep the cost of living stable. For a Swiss company that relies on imported raw materials—say, a chocolate maker importing cocoa beans or a pharmaceutical firm importing chemical precursors—the strong franc is a blessing. It lowers their production costs, giving them a crucial advantage.

But then there is the other side of the coin, and it is a heavy one. This is the world of the Swiss exporter, the engine room of the national economy. Imagine you run a highly skilled company that manufactures precision medical devices. Your factory, your engineers, and your workers are all in Switzerland. You pay their salaries, your rent, and your taxes in Swiss francs. Your costs are locked into the world's strongest currency. However, you sell your devices to hospitals in Germany, France, and the United States. Your customers pay you in euros and dollars.

Every time the franc strengthens, you face a gut-wrenching choice. If the franc gains 10% against the euro, you either have to raise your prices by 10% in Europe—and risk losing your customers to a competitor—or you have to accept 10% less revenue in francs for the same amount of work. Your profit margins get vaporized. This isn't a theoretical problem; it's an existential threat. This relentless pressure is the primary driver behind the fear of "deindustrialization." A company might eventually decide the struggle is no longer worth it. It might keep its headquarters and research labs in Switzerland but move its actual manufacturing—and the jobs that go with it—to a country within the Eurozone, like Slovakia or Germany, simply to align its costs with its revenues.

The "Francogeddon" of January 2015 was the ultimate stress test. When the SNB dropped the exchange rate floor, it was like a dam breaking. The immediate shockwave tore through the Swiss export sector. Business confidence plummeted. As the source text notes, the situation for Swiss manufacturers deteriorated almost overnight, a stark contrast to the optimism felt by their German neighbors. The stock market told the same story: the companies hurt the most were those with the biggest international footprint. But even businesses focused entirely on the domestic market felt the chill, as they suddenly faced a new wave of cheaper competition from imported goods.

And yet, the Swiss economy did not collapse. It bent, but it did not break. This reveals the secret to Swiss resilience. The country has consistently run a massive current account surplus, which is a fancy way of saying it sells far more to the world than it buys from it, year after year. How is this possible under such currency pressure?

The answer lies in the nature of what Switzerland sells. Many Swiss exports are not things you buy because they are cheap; you buy them because they are the best. They are high-value, highly specialized goods that are less sensitive to price. If you need a specific life-saving cancer drug from Roche or a unique piece of machinery from ABB that no one else makes, a 10% price change might not be the deciding factor. The same goes for the luxury watch industry. A person buying a Patek Philippe is not comparison shopping based on currency fluctuations; they are buying a piece of art, a status symbol, and a marvel of engineering. This focus on quality, innovation, and brand power gives the Swiss export sector a built-in shock absorber. It's a testament to a long-term economic strategy that has prioritized being indispensable over being the cheapest.

3.4 The Accountability and Independence of the SNB

To understand the Swiss National Bank, you must first grasp a fundamental concept in modern economics: central bank independence. Think of it like the judiciary. We want judges to be independent of political pressure so they can apply the law fairly. Similarly, we want central bankers to be independent so they can manage the economy for the long-term good of the country, rather than for the short-term political goals of a government facing an election. The SNB is a textbook example of this principle, operating with a level of autonomy that is the envy of many central banks around the world. This independence is not just a tradition; it is written into the nation's constitution.

This freedom allows the SNB to make tough, often unpopular, decisions—like introducing negative interest rates—with a single-minded focus on its mandate: ensuring price stability and serving the general interest of Switzerland. This operational fortress has been the bedrock of the franc's credibility. Investors trust the SNB because they know it won't be forced by politicians to suddenly print money to finance government spending, the classic recipe for currency collapse.

However, the extraordinary challenges of the last two decades have forced the SNB to use tools that stretch the very definition of monetary policy, pushing this independence into a murky and controversial new territory. The problem is its balance sheet. To hold the franc down, the SNB had to print trillions of francs and use them to buy foreign currencies. But it can't just let that money sit there. It has to invest it.

The result is staggering. The Swiss National Bank has been transformed from a traditional central bank into one of the largest asset managers on the planet. Its foreign reserve portfolio is a colossal fund, worth hundreds of billions of dollars. This isn't just government bonds. The SNB is a massive global stock investor. It owns billions of dollars' worth of shares in Apple, Microsoft, Amazon, and other major U.S. technology companies.

This raises profound questions about accountability that go far beyond interest rates. First, there is the issue of financial risk. By becoming a giant hedge fund, the SNB has exposed the Swiss confederation—and by extension, its taxpayers—to the volatility of global stock markets. A major crash on Wall Street could wipe out tens of billions from the SNB's balance sheet overnight. While it has proven to be a savvy investor so far, the risk is immense and is shouldered by an entire nation.

Second, and perhaps more importantly, there is the question of democratic legitimacy. Who decides what the SNB should invest in? Should a public institution, even an independent one, be a top shareholder in Big Tech? What if it invests in companies whose activities conflict with Swiss foreign policy or environmental goals? These are not monetary policy questions; they are deeply political and ethical ones.

This is where the structure of Swiss governance becomes critical. As the source material points out, the SNB operates in an environment of broad public consensus and respect. Unlike the European Central Bank, which is constantly grilled and challenged by a diverse and often skeptical European Parliament, the SNB faces much less intense public scrutiny. The Swiss system relies heavily on the belief that the experts at the SNB know what they are doing.

This consensus has been a source of incredible strength, allowing the SNB to act decisively when needed. But it also highlights a growing tension in modern democracies. The tools needed to manage a 21st-century economy have become so powerful and complex that they blur the lines between technocratic management and political power. The SNB's journey shows that independence, while essential, is not a simple shield. When a central bank's actions involve owning a slice of the world's largest companies, the debate must evolve from if it should be independent to what the limits of that independent power should be and to whom it is ultimately answerable.

Commodity Cycles and the Role of a Floating Exchange Rate: The Australian Experience

4.1 A History of Australia's Commodity Booms and Busts

Australia's story is, in many ways, a story written in the earth itself. Its economic heartbeat has long been dictated by the rhythm of global demand for the vast mineral and agricultural wealth buried beneath its sunburnt soil and sprawling across its plains. This isn't a recent phenomenon; it's the foundational narrative of the nation's prosperity, a tale of spectacular booms that built cities and fortunes, followed by sobering busts that tested the country's resilience.

The first truly transformative chapter began not with coal or iron, but with a glittering discovery: gold. The gold rushes of the 1850s were an explosion of activity that fundamentally reshaped the British colonies. News of easily found nuggets in Victoria and New South Wales sparked a global frenzy. Hundreds of thousands of fortune-seekers from Europe, China, and North America packed onto ships for the long journey south. This massive wave of immigration was a demographic shockwave, tripling Australia's population in just a decade. Cities like Melbourne ballooned almost overnight from small settlements into grand Victorian metropolises, their ornate buildings financed by the incredible wealth being pulled from the ground. This boom wasn't just about the gold itself; it was about building a nation around it. It spurred the development of infrastructure, agriculture to feed the growing population, and a nascent manufacturing sector. But like all booms, it couldn't last. As the alluvial, or surface-level, gold was exhausted, the fever subsided, leaving behind a permanently larger, more complex, and more multicultural society.

Fast-forwarding through the decades, the 20th century brought its own cycles. After the Second World War, the 1950s delivered the "wool boom." With the world rebuilding and economies recovering, demand for Australian wool—then the country's dominant export—skyrocketed, famously allowing Australia to "ride on the sheep's back." The income surge was immense, but it also brought challenges, stoking inflation and creating economic distortions. Another significant surge occurred in the 1970s, this time driven by energy and minerals. The global oil shocks of that decade made Australian coal a highly sought-after commodity, while Japan's post-war industrial miracle created a voracious appetite for iron ore and other resources.

Yet, none of these past episodes could compare to the sheer scale and impact of the "super-cycle" that began in the early 2000s. This boom was, in a word, about China. As the world's most populous nation underwent a once-in-a-millennium industrial and urban transformation, it needed staggering quantities of raw materials to build its cities, railways, and factories. Australia, with its high-quality iron ore and coal reserves located relatively close by, was perfectly positioned to supply this demand.

The result was an economic tidal wave. Commodity prices soared to historic, dizzying heights. Australia's terms of trade—a measure of what it can buy on the global market with the goods it sells—reached levels not seen in over a century. The numbers were breathtaking. Investment in the mining sector, particularly in the vast, remote landscapes of Western Australia and Queensland, exploded. Billions of dollars were poured into digging massive open-cut mines, building new railways, and expanding ports to get the resources out of the ground and onto ships bound for Asia. This created a phenomenon often described as a "two-speed economy." The resource-rich states were booming, with high wages, labor shortages, and soaring property prices. Meanwhile, other parts of the country, particularly those reliant on manufacturing, tourism, or education, struggled under the pressure of a high Australian dollar, which made their goods and services more expensive for the rest of the world.

But the fundamental law of cycles is that what goes up must eventually come down. By around 2012, the boom's peak had passed. China's economic growth began to slow and shift its focus away from heavy industry toward consumption and services. At the same time, the massive global investments in new mines, spurred by the high prices, started to come online, leading to a glut of supply. Prices for iron ore and coal tumbled from their extraordinary peaks. The investment phase of the boom ended, leaving a painful hangover. Mining projects were shelved, construction workers were laid off, and government budgets, which had grown fat on mining royalties and taxes, suddenly faced massive deficits. This bust phase presented Australia with a monumental economic challenge: how to transition away from the engine of mining investment without falling into a deep recession.

4.2 The Floating Australian Dollar as an Automatic Stabilizer

Navigating the violent ups and downs of commodity cycles has always been Australia's great economic puzzle. For much of its history, the country operated under a fixed or managed exchange rate system. This meant the value of the Australian dollar was pegged to another currency, like the British pound or the US dollar. This approach provided a sense of stability, but it was a brittle one. When a commodity boom hit, the fixed exchange rate acted like a blocked pressure valve. The influx of foreign money would swell the domestic money supply, overheat the economy, and send inflation soaring. The only way to adjust was through slow and painful changes in domestic wages and prices. During a bust, the system was even worse, often forcing the government into a painful currency devaluation that shattered confidence and wiped out savings.

This all changed on a momentous day in December 1983. The government of Bob Hawke, with Paul Keating as Treasurer, made the audacious decision to "float" the Australian dollar. It was a seismic shift. From that day forward, the value of the Aussie dollar would not be decided by politicians or central bankers in a back room, but by the relentless, 24/7 forces of global supply and demand. This decision is now almost universally seen as the single most important economic reform in the country's modern history because it handed Australia a powerful, built-in shock absorber.

The genius of the floating dollar lies in its automatic, self-correcting mechanism. It leans against the prevailing economic winds, smoothing out the highs and lows of the commodity cycle. Think of how it worked during the China-driven mining boom. As China paid billions for Australian iron ore, it first had to buy billions of Australian dollars. This massive surge in demand for the AUD pushed its value up dramatically, at one point soaring above parity with the US dollar. This stronger dollar had several crucial, stabilizing effects. Firstly, it made imported goods—from cars and electronics to clothing and food—much cheaper for Australian consumers. This spread the benefits of the mining boom across the entire population and, critically, acted as a powerful brake on inflation. While the mining sector was running hot, the rest of the economy was enjoying lower prices. Secondly, the high dollar made Australia's other exports, like tourism, international education, and manufacturing, more expensive and less competitive. While this was undoubtedly painful for those sectors, it was a necessary part of the adjustment, helping to prevent the entire economy from overheating.

Then, when the commodity bust arrived after 2011 and export prices collapsed, the floating dollar performed its second act. The mechanism simply went into reverse. With less foreign money chasing Australian exports, the demand for the AUD plummeted, and the exchange rate fell significantly. This depreciation worked like a safety net for the economy. Suddenly, Australian exports became much cheaper and more attractive to the rest of the world. A holiday on the Great Barrier Reef became a bargain for American tourists. A degree at an Australian university became more affordable for a student from India. A bottle of Australian wine became more competitive on a shelf in London. This boosted the non-mining parts of the economy right at the moment they needed it most. It encouraged a switching of resources and labor out of the declining mining construction sector and into these recovering industries. This automatic rebalancing allowed the Australian economy to transition away from the mining boom without the deep, prolonged recession that many observers had feared, and which its history suggested was inevitable. The floating exchange rate didn't eliminate the pain of the adjustment, but it cushioned the fall and made the transition dramatically smoother than it ever could have been under a fixed-rate regime. It has become the silent, ever-present stabilizer at the heart of Australia's modern economic management.

4.3 The Reserve Bank of Australia's Policy Response During the Mining Boom

When the mining super-cycle hit Australia in the early 2000s, it wasn't just a wave of prosperity; it was a complex, raging economic storm. For the nation's central bank, the Reserve Bank of Australia (RBA), this was the ultimate test of the modern policy framework it had so carefully constructed. The RBA's job is to keep the Australian economy on an even keel, primarily by targeting a stable, low rate of inflation. But the boom threatened to rip the economy in two. It created what became famously known as a "two-speed" or "multi-speed" economy, and navigating it was one of the most delicate balancing acts in the central bank's history.

On one side, you had the fast lane. This was the Australia directly connected to the boom: the mining companies in Western Australia and Queensland, the engineering firms that built the infrastructure, and the thousands of workers who flocked to the remote mine sites for sky-high wages. This part of the economy was running red hot. The sheer scale of investment was creating bottlenecks, driving up the cost of skilled labor and materials, and pouring a torrent of money into the economy. This was the classic recipe for a dangerous inflationary outbreak.

On the other side, you had the slow lane. This was the rest of Australia. For a manufacturer in Melbourne, a tourism operator in Cairns, or a farmer in New South Wales, the boom felt very different. The very same force lifting the mining sector—a soaring Australian dollar—was acting like a ball and chain on them. Their products and services were becoming prohibitively expensive for overseas customers. Tourists thought twice about visiting, international students looked at other countries, and factories found it impossible to compete with cheaper imports. They weren't just missing out on the party; they were actively being squeezed by it.

So, what could the RBA do? Its primary tool is the official cash rate—the interest rate that influences the cost of borrowing across the entire economy. If it left rates low to help the struggling manufacturers and tourism operators, it risked letting the inflation genie out of the bottle in the booming sectors, which could infect the whole economy. If it jacked up interest rates aggressively to stamp out the inflation threat, it risked crushing the life out of the already struggling non-mining businesses, potentially causing a deep recession in large parts of the country.

The RBA chose a middle path of careful, measured action. It recognized that the primary threat was inflation. A key lesson from Australia's past booms and busts was that letting inflation get out of control was a recipe for a much harder crash later on. So, the RBA began to methodically raise the cash rate. This made it more expensive for businesses to borrow and for households to take out mortgages, acting as a brake on spending and cooling domestic demand. This was a direct, conventional response to the overheating pressures.

Crucially, however, the RBA was not acting alone. It had a powerful partner: the floating Australian dollar. As the RBA raised interest rates, it made Australia an even more attractive place for global investors to park their money, pushing the dollar even higher. This high dollar, while painful for exporters, was a massive help in the fight against inflation. It made all imported goods cheaper, putting downward pressure on prices in shops across the country. In this way, the RBA's interest rate hikes and the currency's natural appreciation worked in tandem. Together, they managed to keep a lid on inflation far more effectively than in any previous commodity boom in

Australia's history, preventing the kind of destructive wage-price spiral that had caused so much damage in the past.

Then, as the boom inevitably peaked and began to unwind, the RBA's role completely reversed. As mining investment projects were completed or cancelled, a massive engine of economic growth sputtered and died. The great challenge now was to avoid a "hard landing." This is where the flexibility of the modern framework truly shone. The RBA began to cut the cash rate, and it did so decisively, eventually taking it to then-historic lows. This made borrowing cheaper, encouraging businesses outside of mining to invest and households to spend, stimulating the weaker parts of the economy. And once again, the floating dollar was the perfect ally. As commodity prices fell and interest rates were cut, the Aussie dollar depreciated significantly, providing a much-needed boost to those long-suffering tourism, education, and manufacturing sectors. The RBA's independent, forward-looking strategy—raising rates on the way up and cutting them on the way down—was the critical human intervention that, alongside the automatic stabilization of the currency, allowed Australia to navigate the biggest resources boom in its history and come out the other side without a recession.

4.4 The Social and Economic Impacts of a Resource-Intensive Economy

The story of Australia's mining boom is often told in grand, national terms: record export values, a soaring dollar, and a surge in national income. But beneath these headline figures lies a far more complex and deeply personal story of how this wave of wealth reshaped Australian society, creating clear winners but also significant losers. While the boom undeniably made the country richer as a whole, the benefits were not spread evenly, and the sheer force of the economic shift left deep and lasting scars on parts of the nation.

The most direct negative impact was the "crowding out" effect on other industries. This wasn't a malicious act, but an unavoidable consequence of economic gravity. The booming mining sector was like a massive new planet in the economic solar system, and its gravitational pull warped everything around it. It needed two things above all else: capital (money for investment) and skilled labor. And it could pay top dollar for both. This meant other sectors had to compete for the same pool of workers and investment funds. A construction company trying to build a new hospital in Sydney found itself competing for engineers and project managers with a multi-billion dollar gas project in Western Australia. The result? Higher costs and labor shortages for everyone else.

But the most powerful force of this crowding-out was the high Australian dollar. For a manufacturing business that had been successfully exporting for decades, the strong dollar was a death sentence. Their products suddenly became 20%, 30%, or even 40% more expensive on the world market, not because of any drop in quality or efficiency, but purely due to currency movements. At the same time, imported goods became dirt cheap, flooding the domestic market. Many businesses, unable to compete, were forced to shrink, lay off loyal, long-serving staff, and in many cases, shut their doors for good. The hollowing out of Australia's manufacturing sector was dramatically accelerated by the boom, creating deep pockets of unemployment and social dislocation in traditional industrial heartlands.

Furthermore, a great paradox of the boom was that while mining dominated Australia's exports, it is a surprisingly small employer. The industry is incredibly capital-intensive, relying on gigantic, expensive machinery rather than a large workforce. At its peak, mining employed only about 2% of all Australian workers. This created a profound disconnect: the sector driving the national narrative was one that the vast majority of Australians had no direct connection to.

This led to uncomfortable questions about who was actually benefiting. A significant portion of the Australian mining industry—estimated to be over 80%—is foreign-owned. This means that while the boom generated astronomical profits, a large share of that money didn't stay in Australia. It flowed offshore to shareholders in London, Zurich, or New York. Of course, the industry did contribute significantly through taxes and royalty payments to the government, which helped fund schools and hospitals. However, fierce public debate erupted over whether this contribution was enough. Complicated tax laws and claims of government subsidies led many to argue that the Australian public was not getting its fair share of the profits being extracted from the nation's non-renewable natural wealth.

Finally, the boom carved new divisions into the social and geographic landscape of the country. It created enormous regional disparities. In mining towns in the Pilbara region of Western Australia, house prices and rents skyrocketed to levels seen in the most exclusive parts of Sydney, and an average worker could earn a six-figure salary. Yet, just a few hundred kilometers away, in a town reliant on agriculture or tourism, communities could be struggling with the consequences of the high dollar. This created a sense of two Australias, fueling social tension and a feeling that the prosperity was happening "somewhere else."

Part II: The Politics and Practice of Fiscal Policy

The Politics of Fiscal Space: Germany's Pivot from Austerity to Stimulus

The Politics of Fiscal Space: Germany's Pivot from Austerity to Stimulus

Germany's economic policy has long been an anchor of European fiscal conservatism, deeply rooted in a unique intellectual tradition and a historical aversion to debt and inflation. Its advocacy for strict fiscal rules has shaped the architecture of the Eurozone. However, in 2025, faced with economic stagnation and new geopolitical imperatives, Germany undertook a historic fiscal pivot. This chapter analyzes this dramatic shift, exploring the tension between the country's ingrained policy doctrines, its pressing economic needs, and the constraints of the very European fiscal framework it was instrumental in creating.
5.1 The Ordoliberal Legacy and the "Debt Brake" (Schuldenbremse)

To understand modern German fiscal policy, one must first understand the intellectual tradition of Ordoliberalism. It's not just an economic theory; for many Germans, it's a core part of their national identity. Emerging in the 1930s and 1940s at the University of Freiburg, Ordoliberalism is a variant of liberalism that emphasizes the need for a strong state to create and enforce a clear, rules-based order (Ordnung) for the market economy to function effectively and humanely. This wasn't about the government leaving the economy alone. Quite the opposite. It was about the government acting as a firm but fair referee, setting the rules of the game and making sure everyone played by them.

Unlike the laissez-faire liberalism popular in Anglo-American countries, Ordoliberalism sees a crucial role for the state in preventing monopolies and ensuring fair competition. It's deeply skeptical of big corporations or powerful unions distorting the market. But unlike Keynesianism, which advocates for government spending to manage the ups and downs of the business cycle, Ordoliberalism is deeply suspicious of such discretionary intervention. The architects of this philosophy, figures like Walter Eucken and Franz Böhm, had lived through the chaos of the Weimar Republic. They witnessed firsthand how hyperinflation could wipe out savings, destroy the middle class, and tear society apart. They also saw the subsequent Nazi command economy, where the state controlled everything. Their philosophy was a direct answer to these twin traumas. The goal was to create stability above all else—a predictable economic environment where people could plan for the future without fearing that the value of their money would suddenly evaporate. This philosophy became the bedrock of West Germany's post-war "social market economy," a model that successfully combined capitalist dynamism with a strong social safety net.

This deep-seated belief in rules-based policy and fiscal prudence was constitutionally enshrined in 2009 with the introduction of the Schuldenbremse, or "debt brake." This was a truly remarkable step. The rule amended the German constitution, its Basic Law, to limit the federal government's structural (cyclically adjusted) budget deficit to a mere 0.35% of GDP. It also required the sixteen federal states (Länder) to run structurally balanced budgets, meaning they couldn't, in normal times, spend more than they took in. The debt brake was more than just a fiscal rule; it was the legal manifestation of a national economic ideology. It was a promise made to future generations that they would not be burdened with the debts of the present. This ideology also heavily influenced Germany's approach to European integration. In Brussels, German officials consistently championed the creation of strict, rules-based fiscal frameworks for the Eurozone, most notably the Stability and Growth Pact (SGP). This often put them at odds with more pragmatically-oriented member states like France and Italy, who saw Germany's obsession with rules as rigid and counterproductive, especially during economic downturns. For Germany, however, these rules were seen as the essential glue holding the single currency together, preventing profligate spending in one country from jeopardizing the stability of the entire bloc.

5.2 The 2025 Fiscal "Shakeup": A Paradigm Shift

After years of sluggish growth and mounting criticism, the dam of German fiscal orthodoxy finally broke in March 2025. The government announced a dramatic overhaul of its fiscal policy, a move quickly dubbed the "fiscal shakeup" (fiskalische Erschütterung) by the media. This represented a clear and stunning break with the long-standing tradition of austerity, paving the way for the largest increase in public spending in a generation. The mood in the country had been shifting for some time. People saw crumbling bridges, experienced chronically delayed trains, and knew that the country's internet speeds were lagging far behind its neighbors. The promise of balanced budgets felt hollow when the foundations of the country's prosperity were visibly eroding.

The new package included three significant and almost revolutionary changes. First was the creation of a new €500 billion off-budget infrastructure investment fund, a clever workaround to the debt brake's strict limitations. This fund, named the "Germany-Fund," was designed to channel massive investment into digitalization, the green energy transition, and public transport over the next decade. Second, the government declared an exemption from the debt brake for defense spending above 1% of GDP. This was a direct response to the new security reality in Europe, acknowledging that protecting the nation was a core constitutional duty that could not be constrained by borrowing limits. Finally, the package included a loosening of the net borrowing cap for the federal states, giving them more flexibility to invest in local schools, hospitals, and infrastructure.

This historic pivot was not driven by a sudden intellectual conversion to Keynesian demand management. The finance minister was careful to state that the government still believed in sound public finances. Rather, it was a pragmatic and reluctant response to two powerful and unavoidable pressures. The first was geopolitical. The shifting landscape in Eastern Europe created an urgent, undeniable need for rearmament and a significant increase in defense spending. The national consensus was clear: Germany could no longer afford to neglect its military. This was a matter of national security, a priority that simply could not be met within the tight constraints of the existing debt brake.

Second, Germany's vaunted export-led growth model had been faltering for several years. The economy had actually contracted in the previous year, and the country was facing enormous investment needs to stay competitive in a changing world. The reliance on selling high-quality machinery and cars to the world was no longer a guaranteed recipe for success. The country needed to modernize its digital infrastructure, accelerate its shift to renewable energy, and upgrade its public services. This confluence of external security threats and internal economic weakness created the political momentum to override a deeply entrenched economic ideology. It was a powerful lesson in policymaking: even the most rigid ideological commitments can be superseded when they clash with what are perceived as core national interests of security and economic prosperity. The Bundesbank, Germany's famously hawkish central bank, acknowledged in a public statement the necessary stimulative effect of this new spending. However, true to its nature, it also issued a stern warning, remaining deeply cautious about the long-term evolution of government debt and the potential risks for inflation. The German shakeup had begun, but its final consequences remained to be seen.

5.3 The Collision Course: German Policy vs. EU Fiscal Rules

Germany's domestic policy shift has created a profound and deeply ironic dilemma at the heart of the European Union. For decades, Berlin was the continent's undisputed champion of fiscal discipline, the strict teacher who insisted everyone else do their homework. Now, that same teacher is not only failing to do their own but is effectively rewriting the assignment. The new fiscal trajectory, which will see Germany's debt-to-GDP ratio rise from its current 67%—already above the 60% EU threshold—is in direct contradiction with the spirit and letter of the EU's recently reformed fiscal framework. This framework, which Germany itself heavily influenced, demands that member states with debt levels above the threshold put them on a clear downward path. Germany is about to do the exact opposite.

This places the European Commission in an almost impossible position. Imagine being the referee in a game where the person who wrote the rulebook suddenly commits a flagrant foul. What do you do? The Commission cannot easily grant an exception to Germany without completely shattering the credibility of the entire rulebook. That rulebook was the product of a painstaking, multi-year negotiation with all 27 member states. If its chief architect is allowed to ignore it, why should anyone else follow it? It would be seen as a blatant case of "one rule for thee, and another for me," confirming the worst suspicions of smaller member states. On the other hand, sanctioning Germany is almost politically unthinkable. It would trigger a monumental political crisis between Brussels and its most powerful member state, paralyzing the Union at a time of immense geopolitical fragility.

This situation, where the rule-maker has become the rule-breaker, exposes a fundamental tension that has always existed in the Eurozone's economic governance. The EU's fiscal rules were largely designed to export German Ordoliberal preferences for stability and debt reduction to the rest of the continent. They were built on the assumption that what was good for Germany was good for Europe. Now, those very rules are constraining Germany itself as it confronts urgent national challenges of security and economic renewal. As analysts from the influential think tank Bruegel have pointed out, this conundrum may be unsolvable without another fundamental reform of the EU rules themselves. Germany's U-turn, born of necessity, has inadvertently provided a powerful political opening for other member states. Leaders in Paris and Rome, who have long chafed under what they see as a rigid, austerity-focused framework, now have the perfect case study. They can argue, with considerable justification, that the rules must be permanently changed. They will push for a system that allows for more flexibility and actively prioritizes strategic public investment in defense, green technology, and digitalization across the entire bloc. In a remarkable turn of events, Germany, the long-time enforcer of fiscal austerity, may have become the unwilling catalyst for dismantling the very system it spent decades building.

5.4 Spillover Effects: The Impact of German Stimulus on the Eurozone

When the Eurozone's largest economy changes course so dramatically, it doesn't just make waves at home; it creates a tide that lifts or lowers boats across the entire continent. A fiscal expansion in Germany stimulates demand not just for German goods and services, but for those of the entire bloc. This happens primarily through the simple, powerful channel of trade. As the German government injects hundreds of billions into infrastructure and defense, German companies need more raw materials, more components, and more machinery. German workers, feeling more secure in their jobs, might spend more on vacations in Spain or on cheese from France. This increased demand acts as a direct economic stimulus for Germany's neighbors.

The numbers are significant. Economic models estimate that a sustained increase in the German fiscal deficit of 1.5% of GDP could boost the Eurozone's overall GDP by a solid 0.4 to 0.5 percentage points by the end of 2026. That might not sound like much, but in the context of a large, mature economy, it represents hundreds of billions of euros in new activity and hundreds of thousands of jobs. The European Commission's own simulations project that the new €500 billion infrastructure fund alone could lift the EU's total GDP by as much as 0.75% by 2035. Crucially, about one-third of this impact would come from these positive spillovers, benefiting other member states directly. For a country like Poland, whose manufacturing sector is deeply integrated with Germany's, or Austria, which shares strong economic and cultural ties, this German stimulus could feel like a welcome tailwind.

However, this dynamic also perfectly illustrates the complex interplay between national fiscal policy and the Eurozone's single monetary policy. A significant fiscal stimulus by the largest member acts as a de facto stimulus for the entire currency area. This, in turn, fundamentally alters the macroeconomic outlook for the European Central Bank (ECB) in Frankfurt. The ECB's job is to manage inflation and growth for the whole bloc, not just one country. Faced with stronger growth and potentially higher inflation than it was previously forecasting, the ECB would be forced to recalibrate. Its carefully laid plans might have to change. Indeed, much analysis suggests that the German stimulus could lead the ECB to pursue a less accommodative policy. This means it might reduce its planned cycle of interest rate cuts in 2025 or even consider raising them sooner than expected. The ECB itself has already acknowledged this German fiscal loosening as a clear "upside risk" to its economic outlook. This case study, therefore, highlights a core reality of the single currency: the sovereign fiscal decisions of one large country can have profound and direct implications for the monetary conditions—the cost of borrowing for families and businesses—experienced by all members of the union.

The Challenges of Fiscal Federalism: Intergovernmental Transfers in Canada

6.1 The Historical Evolution of Canada's Fiscal Federalism

Canada's story is, in many ways, a story of negotiation. It's a constant conversation between a central, federal government and its powerful, distinct provincial partners. The financial relationship between these two levels of government, known as fiscal federalism, is the engine room of that conversation, and its history is a fascinating journey from a centralized dream to a decentralized reality.

It all began in 1867 with the British North America Act. The Fathers of Confederation looked south at the American Civil War, a brutal conflict they believed was caused by an excess of "states' rights," and decided Canada would be different. They envisioned a strong, dominant federal government in Ottawa holding most of the important powers and, crucially, the most lucrative revenue sources, like customs duties and excise taxes. Provinces were given responsibilities that seemed less significant at the time: local works, property, healthcare, and education. It was a design for a centralized nation.

But history rarely follows a blueprint. Almost immediately, the tide began to turn. A series of influential court rulings, many from the Judicial Committee of the Privy Council in London (then Canada's highest court of appeal), began interpreting the constitution in a way that consistently favored provincial powers. These decisions chipped away at federal dominance, reinforcing the provinces' control over their designated areas. Simultaneously, the world was changing. The very responsibilities that seemed minor in

1867—health, education, and social welfare—were about to become the most important, and most expensive, functions of a modern government. The balance of power was quietly, but inexorably, shifting.

The Great Depression of the 1930s shattered the illusion that the original system could work. It was a national crisis that the provinces were constitutionally responsible for managing. They were on the front lines, tasked with providing relief to a desperate and unemployed populace, but their limited taxing powers meant their wallets were empty. They simply could not cope. The financial mismatch was laid bare for all to see: the level of government with the greatest social responsibility had the least capacity to raise money. This near-collapse of provincial finances led to the creation of the landmark Rowell-Sirois Commission in 1937. The commission undertook a sweeping review of the country's economic and financial structure and came to a clear conclusion: the federal government had to step in. It proposed that Ottawa take over responsibility for unemployment insurance and that it be given the exclusive power to levy personal and corporate income taxes, in return providing the provinces with national adjustment grants to ensure a basic standard of services across the country.

While the outbreak of World War II put these grand recommendations on hold, the intellectual die was cast. The commission had fundamentally reshaped the way Canadians thought about their federation. It planted the idea that every Canadian, no matter which province they lived in, was entitled to a reasonably similar level of government service.

The post-war era brought this idea to life. A wave of prosperity and a new social conscience led to a massive expansion of the welfare state. Universal healthcare, postsecondary education support, and comprehensive social assistance programs became pillars of the Canadian identity. But these were all provincial responsibilities. Provincial spending began to skyrocket, quickly outpacing federal expenditures. A fundamental imbalance was now entrenched: Ottawa had the superior power to collect taxes, but the provinces had the ever-growing spending obligations.

The solution was the creation of a complex, sprawling, and perpetually debated system of intergovernmental transfers. Think of it as a form of plumbing for the nation's finances, redirecting revenue from the federal collector to the provincial spenders. These transfers have worn many different hats over the decades. In the beginning, there were programs like the Canada Assistance Plan (CAP), where Ottawa agreed to pay for 50% of eligible provincial spending on welfare and social services. This was a cost-sharing model that, while generous, was criticized for giving the federal government a "blank cheque" and for creating an incentive for provinces to spend more, knowing Ottawa would foot half the bill.

Later, the system evolved towards "block funding." Arrangements like the Established Programs Financing (EPF) bundled money for health and education into a single lump-sum transfer, giving provinces more flexibility in how they spent the funds. The modern system is even more streamlined, with two major block transfers: the Canada Health Transfer (CHT) and the Canada Social Transfer (CST). This journey has never been a smooth one. It has been defined by tense federal-provincial negotiations, arguments over funding levels, disputes over whether Ottawa can attach "strings" or conditions to the money, and a constant struggle to define who is accountable to the taxpayer. This dynamic tension is not a flaw in the system; it is the system itself, a continuous dialogue that shapes the Canadian experience.

6.2 The Equalization Program: Mechanics and Controversies

At the very heart of Canada's complex fiscal machinery lies a single, powerful idea: fairness. This idea is given life through the Equalization program, a uniquely Canadian invention that has become the cornerstone of the country's approach to national unity and shared citizenship. It is arguably the most important, and certainly the most controversial, intergovernmental transfer.

First introduced in 1957 and later enshrined in the Constitution in 1982, the program's purpose is both simple and profound. The constitution commits Parliament to the principle of making equalization payments "to ensure that provincial governments have sufficient revenues to provide reasonably comparable levels of public services at reasonably comparable levels of taxation." In simpler terms, it's a promise. It's a promise that the quality of your child's school or your parent's hospital care shouldn't depend dramatically on which province you happen to call home. It aims to smooth out the economic wrinkles that naturally exist across a country as vast and diverse as Canada.

Here's how it works on a basic level. The program is funded entirely by the federal government out of its general tax revenues. It is not a system where wealthy provinces write cheques directly to less-wealthy ones. Instead, Ottawa acts as the intermediary. Each year, a complex formula is used to calculate every province's "fiscal capacity"—a measure of its potential ability to raise revenue. This calculation looks at how much money a province could generate if it applied average national tax rates to its own economy, across five major categories: personal income taxes, business income taxes, consumption taxes (like the GST/HST), property taxes, and revenues from natural resources.

Once each province's per capita fiscal capacity is calculated, it's compared to a national standard—currently, the average of all ten provinces. Provinces that fall below this average are designated "have-not" provinces and receive an Equalization payment from Ottawa to bring them up to the average. Provinces whose fiscal capacity is above the average are called "have" provinces and receive nothing. The total amount of money available for the program grows each year based on a three-year moving average of Canada's economic growth (nominal GDP), making the system predictable for federal budgeting.

This formulaic, rules-based approach is designed to be objective, but in practice, it is the subject of intense and unending political controversy. The single biggest flashpoint has always been the treatment of natural resource revenues. How do you account for the massive, but incredibly volatile, wealth generated by Alberta's oil sands or Newfoundland and Labrador's offshore oil fields without completely skewing the entire system? If you include all of it, a resource boom in one province could cause the national average to skyrocket, meaning almost every other province would suddenly need a massive payment, potentially bankrupting the program. If you exclude it, you aren't accurately measuring a province's true ability to pay for its own services. Canada has tried numerous solutions over the years—excluding some resource revenues, including only a portion, or implementing caps—but no answer has ever satisfied everyone. This issue fuels sentiments of Western alienation, particularly in Alberta, where many feel they contribute a disproportionate amount to the national coffers without receiving fair consideration.

Another deep-seated controversy involves the potential for the program to create "perverse incentives." Critics argue that because Equalization payments decrease as a "have-not" province's own revenues increase, it creates a "welfare trap" that discourages them from developing their own economies. For instance, if a province were to approve a new mine or develop its shale gas reserves, the resulting revenue would be offset by a reduction in its Equalization transfer. This "clawback" can reduce the political and financial motivation to pursue economic growth, creating a cycle of dependency.

Furthermore, the very labels "have" and "have-not" create a divisive political narrative. The list of provinces on either side of the ledger changes over time, and these shifts can cause political earthquakes. When Ontario, long the economic engine of the country, began receiving Equalization payments for the first time after the 2008 financial crisis, it was a profound shock to the system, sparking a national debate about the program's fairness and sustainability. Equalization is more than a fiscal transfer; it is a reflection of Canada's identity, a source of both unity and profound division, and a constant reminder that in a decentralized federation, the question of "who pays for what" is never truly settled.

6.3 The Economic Consequences of Intergovernmental Transfers

Money is never just money. It's a tool, an incentive, a promise, and sometimes, a problem. In Canada, the billions of dollars that flow from the federal government to the provinces through intergovernmental transfers are all of these things at once. The economic consequences of this system are vast, complex, and touch the lives of every single Canadian, creating a constant and delicate balancing act between the virtues of national unity and the vices of economic distortion.

On one side of the ledger, the system is a powerful force for good, acting as the economic glue that helps hold a sprawling and diverse country together. This is its noblest purpose. Equalization, in particular, ensures that a child growing up in rural New Brunswick has access to a quality of education that is not drastically different from that of a child in bustling Calgary. It means a senior needing medical care in Manitoba can expect a standard of service comparable to one in Ontario. Without these transfers, Canada would risk becoming a country of deep and entrenched inequalities. Provinces with smaller economies or fewer natural resources would be trapped in a vicious cycle. To fund basic services, they would have to impose punishingly high tax rates on their citizens and businesses. This, in turn, would drive people and investment away to more prosperous provinces, shrinking their tax base even further and making it even harder to pay for schools, hospitals, and roads. The transfers act as a circuit breaker, stopping this cycle before it starts. They promote a sense of shared citizenship, reinforcing the idea that a Canadian is a Canadian, and that your opportunities in life shouldn't be dictated by the accident of your provincial birthplace.

However, on the other side of the ledger, critics argue that this well-intentioned system creates a web of unintended and often negative economic consequences. A major concern is the thorny issue of accountability. When a provincial government gets a significant chunk of its budget as a no-strings-attached cheque from Ottawa, who is it really accountable to? Local politicians can announce new programs or spending without having to make the difficult decision of raising taxes on their own voters to pay for them. It creates a disconnect. The government that spends the money is not the same government that has to raise it. This can lead to less fiscal discipline and a political culture where it's easier to demand more from a distant federal government than to foster economic growth and efficiency at home.

This leads to the most potent economic critique: the idea that Equalization can create a "welfare trap" for the provinces that receive it. It's a controversial but persistent argument. Imagine you are the premier of a province that receives a large Equalization payment. A company wants to develop a new mine that would create jobs and generate hundreds of millions of dollars in provincial tax revenue. On the surface, this is a clear win. But the Equalization formula is waiting in the background. As your province's own-source revenues go up from that new mine, your Equalization payment from Ottawa will go down. The formula effectively "claws back" a significant portion of your new earnings. This creates what economists call a high marginal effective tax rate on economic development. The incentive to take political risks, to streamline regulations, and to aggressively pursue pro-growth policies is blunted, because a large share of the reward will simply be cancelled out by a smaller transfer payment. It doesn't mean recipient provinces don't want to grow, but it does mean the system can subtly discourage the very activities that would lead to long-term self-sufficiency.

Finally, this entire structure exists under the shadow of a monumental reality: debt. Both the federal government and the provinces are carrying enormous levels of debt. The combined interest payments on this debt are staggering, projected to be over $90 billion for the 2024-2025 fiscal year. This isn't just an abstract number; it's money that cannot be spent on healthcare, childcare, or fighting climate change. It raises profound questions about the long-term sustainability of the current transfer system. How long can a federal government, itself deeply in debt, continue to finance such large-scale transfers to provinces, many of whom are also in precarious financial positions? This fiscal reality is forcing a difficult national conversation. The system of transfers that was designed to ensure equity and stability now faces a fundamental challenge: can it survive in an era of soaring debt and increasing economic uncertainty?

6.4 The Political Economy of Fiscal Negotiations

To understand fiscal federalism in Canada, you have to look beyond the spreadsheets and formulas. You have to see it for what it is: a high-stakes political drama that never truly ends. This isn't a technical exercise carried out by accountants in quiet back rooms. It is a deeply human and intensely political process, driven by negotiation, public posturing, regional pride, and raw power. The distribution of money is the distribution of power, and in Canada, the fight over that distribution is a defining feature of the country's political life.

The main stage for this drama is the federal-provincial conference, often called a First Ministers' Meeting. These gatherings, which bring the Prime Minister and the thirteen provincial and territorial premiers together, are supposed to be forums for collaboration and compromise. More often than not, they become arenas for conflict. The days leading up to them are filled with strategic leaks to the media, as premiers try to frame the narrative and rally public support for their positions. The meetings themselves can be tense affairs, pitting region against region, and the provinces collectively against Ottawa. A premier from a wealthy, resource-rich province like Alberta will arrive with a mandate from their voters to defend their contribution to the federation and fight for "fairness." A premier from a recipient province like Nova Scotia will come armed with arguments about the need for stable funding to protect vital public services. And the Prime Minister sits at the head of the table, tasked with the near-impossible job of balancing these competing interests, controlling federal spending, and somehow holding the country together.

The most intense battles are fought during the legally required five-year review of the fiscal arrangements. This is when the very rules of the game are up for debate. Every province comes with a shopping list. They lobby for tweaks to the Equalization formula that will benefit them—a different way of calculating resource revenues, a change in how tax bases are measured. They argue for massive increases in the Canada Health Transfer, citing the immense pressures of an aging population and rising healthcare costs. It becomes a complex, multi-sided chess match. Provinces will form alliances based on shared interests. The Atlantic provinces might present a united front, while the Western provinces might band together to oppose changes they see as harmful.

This dynamic creates a political environment where the focus can shift from the real-world goal—delivering the best possible services to citizens—to the political game of intergovernmental relations. Success for a premier is often measured not by their policy innovations at home, but by how much money they can extract from Ottawa. It can foster a sense of grievance and division. When provinces are constantly framed as "winners" and "losers" in these negotiations, it erodes national unity. People in "have" provinces can begin to feel that their hard-earned tax dollars are being unfairly redistributed, leading to resentment and fueling regional alienation. At the same time, people in "have-not" provinces can feel that they are being short-changed or that their legitimate needs are being ignored by a distant and uncaring federal government.

The language used is telling. It's often the language of conflict: battles, struggles, fights. This isn't just political rhetoric; it reflects a genuine and deeply felt tension at the core of the Canadian federation. The enduring challenge is to find a way to reform this process. How can Canada maintain the national solidarity that is the very soul of Equalization, while also improving accountability and efficiency? How can the country move from a system that often encourages conflict to one that fosters genuine collaboration? Finding the answer to these questions is one of the great, unfinished projects of Canadian nation-building. It requires more than just better formulas; it requires a renewed commitment to finding common ground, even when it's easier to retreat to the familiar comfort of our regional corners.

Fiscal Policy and Redistribution in a Post-Apartheid Economy: The South African Challenge

7.1 The Economic Legacy of Apartheid and Structural Inequality

To truly grasp the challenge facing South Africa in 1994, one must understand that apartheid was not merely a system of social prejudice. It was a meticulously engineered economic machine, designed with the singular purpose of enriching the white minority by systematically impoverishing and controlling the non-white majority. Its legacy was not a series of unfortunate side effects; the inequality was the entire point. It was an architecture of extraction built over decades, leaving behind a nation that was, in economic terms, two entirely different worlds occupying the same space.

The foundation of this architecture was the brutal and total control of land. The Natives Land Act of 1913 was the cornerstone. With the stroke of a pen, it designated approximately 87% of South Africa's land for the white minority, leaving a mere 13% for the vast black majority. This was not just an act of theft; it was an act of economic strangulation. It destroyed self-sufficient agrarian communities, severed ancestral and spiritual ties to the land, and eliminated the possibility of black individuals accumulating wealth through agriculture. This dispossession created a massive, dependent population with only one thing left to sell: their labor.

This forced dependency was channeled into the so-called "Bantustans" or homelands. These were not viable states; they were fragmented, overpopulated, and economically desolate territories. They were, in essence, holding pens. They lacked industry, infrastructure, and fertile soil, making them incapable of supporting their populations. The design was cynical and brutally effective: men were forced to become migrant workers, leaving their families for months or years at a time to work in the mines, factories, and farms owned by white South Africans. This system tore apart the social fabric of black communities while ensuring a constant, inexhaustible supply of cheap labor to power the nation's industrial engine. By 1985, the combined per capita income in the Bantustans was estimated to be less than 8% of that in the rest of South Africa.

The control extended deep into the labor market itself. The policy of "job reservation" legally barred black workers from holding skilled or semi-skilled positions, reserving them exclusively for whites. This created an artificial ceiling on the economic aspirations of millions. This was powerfully reinforced by the Bantu Education Act of 1953. Its chief architect, Prime Minister Hendrik Verwoerd, was chillingly explicit about its purpose, stating, "There is no place for [the Bantu] in the European community above the level of certain forms of labour... What is the use of teaching the Bantu child mathematics when it cannot use it in practice?" The state deliberately engineered an education system designed to produce a subservient workforce, not a class of innovators, managers, or professionals. The spending disparity was staggering; in the mid-1970s, the state spent more than 10 times more on a white child's education than on a black child's.

By the early 1990s, the cumulative effect of these policies was a society with inequality etched into its very soul. The statistics paint a stark picture of this dualistic economy. In 1994, the average white household income was approximately 12 times that of the average black household. White South Africans, who constituted just over 10% of the population, controlled over 85% of the nation's personal wealth and the vast majority of corporate ownership. The Gini coefficient, a standard measure of income inequality, stood at an estimated 0.68, making South Africa one of the most unequal societies on Earth. Access to basic services was a portrait of this divide: while nearly 100% of white households had electricity and running water, fewer than 20% of black rural households had the same. This was the landscape of economic devastation that the new democratic government inherited—a chasm of disparity, deliberately created and maintained for generations.

7.2 The Post-1994 Fiscal Framework: Balancing Redistribution and Consolidation

When the African National Congress (ANC) came to power in 1994, it stood before a monumental task. On one hand, there was the roaring moral and political mandate to dismantle apartheid's economic structures and deliver a better life for all. The promises of the freedom struggle—houses, security, and comfort—were fresh in the minds of the electorate. On the other hand, the new government inherited an economy that was sputtering, with high inflation, low growth, and a worrying level of public debt, which stood at around 48% of GDP. The challenge was immense: how to redistribute wealth and opportunity on a massive scale without spooking international investors and tipping the country into a fiscal crisis.

The first chapter of this story, from roughly 1994 to 2000, was defined by caution. The government adopted the Growth, Employment, and Redistribution (GEAR) strategy in 1996. GEAR was a largely orthodox economic policy that prioritized fiscal discipline above all else. Its goals were to cut the budget deficit, privatize some state assets, liberalize trade, and bring inflation under control. For many of the government's allies in the trade union movement and the Communist Party, this felt like a bitter pill to swallow, a turn towards the very market-driven policies they had fought against. However, for the government, it was a necessary step to establish credibility. They needed to show the world that the new South Africa would be a responsible manager of its finances. The strategy worked in this regard. The budget deficit was trimmed from over 7% of GDP in the early 90s to under 3%, and a stable macroeconomic foundation was laid. The cost, however, was that the grand-scale redistribution many had hoped for was put on a slower track.

The real shift came in the second phase, from the early 2000s to the eve of the global financial crisis in 2008. This period marked a "golden era" for South Africa's public finances. The prudent management of the GEAR years, combined with a global commodities boom that boosted South Africa's export earnings, led to a surge in tax revenues. The government suddenly had the resources to dramatically ramp up its redistributive efforts without compromising fiscal stability. This is when the modern South African social welfare state truly took shape.

The most powerful tool of redistribution became the social grant system. This system was expanded at an incredible pace. The child support grant, in particular, grew from reaching a few hundred thousand children to over 12 million by the end of the decade. Along with old-age pensions and disability grants, this network of social transfers became a vital lifeline for the country's poorest households. By 2011, nearly a third of the population, over 15 million people, were receiving some form of social grant. Studies showed that these grants were incredibly effective, almost single-handedly cutting the rate of extreme poverty by half and significantly improving nutritional and educational outcomes for children.

Alongside direct cash transfers, the government poured money into services. Millions of RDP (Reconstruction and Development Programme) houses were built. Access to electricity was extended to over 85% of households, up from just 50% in the mid-90s. The number of households with access to clean drinking water saw a similar dramatic increase. This "social wage"—the combination of cash grants and free or subsidized basic services—had a tangible impact on inequality. While the Gini coefficient for market income remained stubbornly high, when the effect of taxes and social spending was factored in, it showed a noticeable reduction. The budget reflected this success; by the 2007/08 fiscal year, South Africa recorded a budget surplus, and its debt-to-GDP ratio had fallen to a low of 27%.

However, this era of fiscal health came to an abrupt end after 2008. The global financial crisis hit South Africa's economy hard, causing growth to plummet and tax revenues to dry up. Simultaneously, the political era of "state capture" and widespread corruption under the Zuma administration began to take hold. State-owned enterprises like the power utility, Eskom, were systematically looted, draining the treasury and requiring massive bailouts. This toxic combination of slowing growth and rampant corruption created a fiscal death spiral. The budget swung from surplus to large, persistent deficits. Public debt began to climb relentlessly, soaring past 70% of GDP in the years that followed. The government that had once had the resources to expand its support for the poor now found itself in a fiscal straitjacket, struggling to maintain existing services while being crushed by rising debt service costs. The dream of the early 2000s had faded, replaced by the grim reality of a state whose capacity to drive redistribution had been severely wounded.

7.3 The Role of Social Grants and Public Services in Mitigating Inequality

In the vast and complex machinery of the post-apartheid state, no tool has been more direct, more powerful, or more impactful in the fight against raw poverty than the social grant system. While economic policies aimed at structural change have often had mixed results, the simple act of putting cash directly into the hands of the poorest South Africans has been nothing short of a revolution. This system, alongside a deliberate focus on pro-poor public services, forms the very core of South Africa's redistributive strategy. It represents the most tangible fulfillment of the promise of 1994 for millions of citizens.

The social grant network is the jewel in the crown of this strategy. It is one of the most extensive and well-targeted social safety nets in the developing world. Its flagship is the Child Support Grant (CSG), a monthly stipend paid to the primary caregiver of a child living in poverty. The growth of this single grant is staggering. From reaching a few hundred thousand children in its infancy, it now supports over 18 million children, making it the largest program by far. For countless households where unemployment is the norm, this small monthly amount is the difference between eating and starving. It is the money that buys maize meal, a pair of school shoes, or the taxi fare to get to a clinic. Its impact goes far beyond simple sustenance; extensive research has shown that children in households receiving the CSG have better nutritional outcomes, are taller and healthier, and are significantly more likely to attend and stay in school.

Equally important is the Old-Age Pension. While it existed before 1994, it was racially skewed, with white pensioners receiving far more than their black counterparts. The democratic government equalized and expanded it, turning it into a pillar of community support. In a country ravaged by unemployment and the HIV/AIDS pandemic, it is often a grandmother's pension that supports an entire multi-generational household, feeding and clothing her grandchildren. The pension has become an engine of local economies, a stable source of income in communities with very few others. Together with the Disability Grant, which provides a lifeline for the most vulnerable, this trinity of grants forms a powerful shield against the absolute destitution that would otherwise engulf millions. The numbers confirm the story: it is estimated that social grants alone have cut the poverty gap—the distance between a poor household's income and the poverty line—by nearly half.

The second arm of this strategy is what is often called the "social wage"—the value of public services provided by the state, which are heavily tilted towards the poor. This is redistribution not in cash, but in kind. The most significant area is education. Post-1994, South Africa enshrined the right to basic education for all. The government established thousands of "no-fee" schools in the country's poorest districts, ensuring that a lack of money would not be a barrier to entry. School feeding schemes were rolled out, providing what is for many children their only guaranteed nutritious meal of the day. As a result, school enrollment rates are now nearly universal.

Similarly, in healthcare, the state built over 1,300 new clinics, mostly in rural and township areas that had been historically neglected. Primary healthcare was made free for pregnant women and young children. For the 84% of the population without private medical insurance, the public health system is their only option. The state also embarked on one of the most ambitious housing and basic service delivery programs in the world. Since 1994, over 3 million free or subsidized houses have been built. The number of households connected to the electricity grid has nearly doubled, and millions more now have access to clean running water and basic sanitation.

However, the immense success of this redistributive push is shadowed by a profound and stubborn limitation. The fiscal system, for all its power, can only redistribute the income that the economy generates. And it is here that the strategy meets its wall. The quality of the "social wage" is often tragically poor. A child may be in school, but if that school lacks proper sanitation, qualified teachers, and basic resources, the education they receive will not equip them to compete in the modern economy. A patient may have access to a clinic, but if it is understaffed and regularly runs out of essential medicines, their health outcomes will suffer. The RDP houses built are often small, of poor quality, and located far from economic opportunities, inadvertently reinforcing apartheid-era spatial divides.

Most fundamentally, this entire redistributive model rests on a dangerously narrow base. It redistributes from the small slice of the population and corporate sector that is formally employed and pays taxes to the massive population that is excluded from the economy. The underlying problem—the catastrophic rate of unemployment—remains unsolved. The social grants and services are a vital, life-saving intervention, but they are a treatment for the symptoms, not a cure for the disease.

7.4 Current Fiscal Challenges: High Debt, Slow Growth, and Social Demands

For all its noble intentions and tangible successes, South Africa's post-apartheid fiscal model has run headfirst into a wall of economic reality. The country is now trapped in a vicious cycle of high debt, stagnant economic growth, and ever-rising social demands. The "fiscal storm" that began brewing after the 2008 global financial crisis has now become a permanent, menacing feature of the political and economic landscape. The delicate balancing act between redistribution and consolidation, so skillfully managed in the early 2000s, has collapsed, leaving policymakers with a set of almost impossible choices.

The core of the problem lies in what experts call the "post-apartheid distributional regime." This is a simple but devastating concept: while the government uses the budget to redistribute money from the rich to the poor through taxes and spending, the underlying structure of the economy continues to produce inequality at a faster rate. The primary engine of this inequality is the labor market. South Africa suffers from one of the highest structural unemployment rates in the world. For the youth, the situation is catastrophic, with unemployment consistently hovering above 60%. This means that the majority of young people leaving school have no prospect of finding a formal job. This single fact is the main driver of poverty and the perpetuation of inequality across generations. Without an income from work, millions of households are completely dependent on the state for survival.

Policies designed to address this structural inequality, such as Black Economic Empowerment (BEE) and affirmative action, have largely failed to shift the needle. While their goal was to de-racialize the economy and bring more black South Africans into the ownership and management of capital, critics argue they have been implemented in a way that benefits only a small, politically connected elite. Instead of fostering broad-based empowerment through new business creation and job growth, these policies have often been reduced to a box-ticking exercise, enriching a few without fundamentally altering the economic exclusion of the masses.

Into this structurally fragile environment came the perfect storm of the last decade. The 2008 financial crisis ended the commodity boom and slammed the brakes on economic growth. Then came the era of "state capture" under the Zuma administration. This was not just corruption; it was the organized, systematic looting of the state's financial resources. Key state-owned enterprises, particularly the electricity utility Eskom, were plundered, leaving them financially bankrupt and operationally broken. The constant need for massive government bailouts to keep these entities afloat became a catastrophic drain on the national treasury. Billions of rand that could have been spent on services or infrastructure were instead used to plug holes created by graft.

The final blow was the COVID-19 pandemic. It forced the government to implement costly lockdowns that crushed the economy while simultaneously requiring massive emergency spending on social relief grants and health services. This combination of factors caused South Africa's public debt to explode. Having fallen to a healthy 27% of GDP in 2008, it has since skyrocketed to over 75% and continues to climb. The consequences are dire. Today, South Africa spends more of its budget on paying interest on its debt than it does on healthcare, economic development, or policing. This is money that creates no jobs and builds no houses; it is simply the cost of past borrowing.

This leaves the government in an impossible bind. On one side, international financial institutions and credit rating agencies demand fiscal consolidation—austerity, spending cuts, and debt stabilization. On the other side, the social reality of mass poverty and inequality creates immense, and legitimate, pressure for more social spending, not less. Cutting the social grant system is politically unthinkable and would trigger a humanitarian crisis. But continuing to borrow to fund the deficit is unsustainable and risks tipping the country into a full-blown debt crisis.

The path forward is incredibly narrow and difficult. It is now clear that the solution cannot be found within the budget alone. The country must urgently engineer a new economic growth strategy—one that is focused on creating mass employment. This means tackling the deep structural constraints, chief among them the crippling electricity crisis caused by the collapse of Eskom. It requires improving the quality of education to produce a skilled workforce and creating a regulatory environment that encourages investment and small business growth. Long-term fiscal sustainability is not a separate goal; it is completely dependent on achieving higher, more inclusive economic growth. Without an economy that creates jobs, the state will simply run out of money to redistribute.

The Macroeconomics of Disintegration: Britain's Fiscal and Monetary Path After Brexit

The Macroeconomics of Disintegration: A Deeper Look

The United Kingdom's departure from the European Union wasn't just a political event; it was a fundamental rewiring of its economic relationships with its closest neighbors and the world. To understand its consequences, we have to look beyond the daily headlines and see Brexit for what it is: a permanent, self-inflicted shock to the nation's economic structure. This analysis explores the deep and lasting impacts of this decision, moving from the theoretical shock to the very real and measurable consequences for how Britain trades, invests, and ultimately, how productive it can be.

8.1 Brexit as a Permanent Negative Supply-Side Shock

Imagine the economy as a car engine. A cyclical downturn, like a recession, is like running low on fuel. It's a serious problem, but you can solve it by adding more fuel—government spending or lower interest rates—and the engine can eventually return to its previous power. A supply-side shock, however, is different. It's like someone has poured sand into the engine itself. The engine's fundamental capacity to perform has been damaged. It can't run as fast or as efficiently as it once did, no matter how much fuel you pump in.

This is the most accurate way to understand Brexit. It wasn't a temporary problem of low demand. Instead, it was a deliberate choice to alter the very mechanics of the UK economy, making the essential processes of production and trade inherently more difficult. This change represents a permanent reduction in the UK's economic potential, or what economists call a negative supply-side shock.

The main source of this economic friction comes not from tariffs—taxes on imported goods—which were largely avoided in the final Trade and Cooperation Agreement (TCA). Instead, the damage stems from the reintroduction of non-tariff barriers (NTBs). For decades, a British company selling goods to Germany faced no more hassle than selling to Scotland. The goods flowed freely, without checks, without extensive paperwork, and without regulatory hurdles. This seamless system, known as the Single Market, was the bedrock of countless business models.

Overnight, that system vanished. It was replaced by a mountain of new logistical and administrative burdens that act as "grit" in the machinery of commerce. Consider a small cheesemaker in Somerset wanting to sell cheddar to a deli in Paris. Before Brexit, the process was simple. After Brexit, that same cheesemaker now needs to complete extensive customs declarations, obtain export health certificates for each shipment (which require a veterinarian's sign-off), and navigate complex "rules of origin" paperwork to prove the cheese is British enough to qualify for zero tariffs. Their French customer, in turn, faces new import procedures. The shipment might be delayed at the border for physical inspection. Every step adds time, cost, and uncertainty.

Now, multiply that single example by hundreds of thousands of businesses, from car manufacturers relying on components arriving from the EU just in time for assembly, to chemical companies whose products need to meet dual sets of UK and EU regulations. This is the pervasive, grinding reality of the new trading relationship. It forces businesses to spend money not on innovation or expansion, but on compliance, logistics, and navigating bureaucracy.

This is why the Office for Budget Responsibility (OBR), the UK's independent economic forecaster, has been so consistent in its assessment. Their conclusion that Brexit will ultimately reduce the UK's long-run productivity by 4% is a stark one. This doesn't mean the economy shrinks by 4% and stops. It means the entire potential growth path of the UK has been lowered. The country will be permanently poorer than it would have been had it remained in the EU. Similarly, the OBR's forecast that UK trade intensity—a measure of how much a country trades relative to its GDP—will be 15% lower is a direct reflection of this new friction. By choosing to leave the world's largest and most integrated trading bloc, the UK has chosen to become a less open, and therefore less dynamic, economy. The shock is permanent because these barriers are now embedded in the legal and logistical framework of UK-EU trade, fundamentally constraining the nation's economic horsepower for the foreseeable future.

8.2 The Impact on Trade, Investment, and Productivity

The theoretical model of a supply-side shock has, in the years since the referendum, played out in the real world with tangible economic consequences. The "grit" in the system has slowed the gears of commerce, and the data on business investment, trade flows, and national productivity tells a clear and consistent story of an economy struggling to adapt to its new, more constrained reality.

The Great Investment Strike

Perhaps the most immediate and damaging economic consequence of Brexit was the profound uncertainty it unleashed. For nearly five years, from the referendum in mid-2016 to the final agreement at the end of 2020, British businesses operated in a fog. They had no idea what the future rules for trade, regulation, or hiring would be. In such an environment, long-term decision-making becomes almost impossible.

Faced with this uncertainty, firms did the most rational thing they could: they paused. They delayed building new factories, held off on purchasing new machinery, and cancelled expansion plans. This phenomenon has been called the "investment strike." Why would a Japanese car company, for example, invest hundreds of millions in upgrading its UK plant when it didn't know if it could sell the cars produced there into the EU market without tariffs or crippling border delays? Why would a UK tech firm build a new data center when it was unsure about future data-sharing rules with the continent?

This wasn't just a brief pause; it was a multi-year drag on the UK's ability to build its productive capacity. The data is sobering. The OBR has consistently pointed out that business investment has been dramatically weaker than in other major economies, failing to recover from the 2016 vote in the way its peers did. Research from institutions like the National Institute of Economic and Social Research (NIESR) put a number on this loss, suggesting business investment was over 12% lower by 2023 than it would have been on its pre-referendum trajectory. This lost investment represents a permanent scarring of the economy. It means fewer modern tools for workers, slower adoption of new technologies, and a weaker foundation for future growth.

The anticipation of the trade barriers proved to be just as harmful as the barriers themselves.

Lagging Trade and the Myth of 'Global Britain'

The impact on trade has been just as evident. While global trade has been volatile due to the pandemic and other disruptions, detailed analysis consistently shows that the UK has underperformed its G7 peers. Since the implementation of the TCA, UK trade in goods with the EU has been particularly weak. While proponents of Brexit envisioned a "Global Britain" pivoting away from Europe to strike lucrative deals with fast-growing economies around the world, this vision has collided with economic gravity.

The simple truth is that trade is overwhelmingly driven by proximity. A country naturally trades most with its nearest neighbors. The EU is not only on the UK's doorstep, it is a bloc of over 450 million wealthy consumers. The economic gains from new Free Trade Agreements (FTAs) with countries like Australia and New Zealand are, by the UK government's own estimates, minuscule in comparison to the losses from erecting new barriers with Europe. The government's own impact assessment, for instance, forecasts that the Australia deal will add somewhere between 0.08% and 0.1% to UK GDP over 15 years. This is a rounding error compared to the estimated 4% long-run GDP loss from leaving the EU. It's like cancelling your most profitable contract and trying to make up for it with a few small, distant clients.

The Productivity Puzzle Solved

The final piece of the puzzle is productivity—the measure of economic output per hour worked. This is the ultimate determinant of a country's living standards. The combination of chronically weak investment and reduced trade openness creates a perfect storm for stagnant productivity.

The link is straightforward. When a country is open to trade with highly advanced economies, its domestic firms are forced to compete. This competitive pressure pushes them to become more innovative, more efficient, and to adopt the best technologies and management practices. Reducing trade with the EU dampens this competitive pressure, allowing less efficient firms to survive and slowing the diffusion of new ideas.

At the same time, the "investment strike" has left British workers with older, less effective tools, software, and machinery compared to their international counterparts. A factory worker with a 15-year-old robot will simply be less productive than one with a state-of-the-art automated system. An accountant using outdated software will be slower than one with the latest cloud-based platform. This is the direct result of years of underinvestment.

Together, these forces explain why the UK's already-poor productivity performance has worsened. The Brexit shock has provided a clear, if unwelcome, answer to Britain's long-standing productivity puzzle. By raising barriers to trade and chilling investment, it has fundamentally weakened the key drivers of efficiency and innovation, setting the country on a path to a less dynamic and less prosperous future.

The Macroeconomics of Disintegration: Policy in a New Reality

The decision to leave the European Union did more than just introduce friction at the borders; it sent deep shockwaves through the very foundations of the UK's economic policymaking. Both the government, which controls taxes and spending (fiscal policy), and the Bank of England, which manages interest rates (monetary policy), have been forced to adapt to a new, harsher reality. They are now navigating a smaller, less efficient economy, a challenge that has reshaped their rulebooks and constrained their choices for the foreseeable future.

8.3 Post-Brexit Fiscal Policy: Navigating a Smaller Economy

Think of the national economy like a large company. The government's tax revenue is the company's annual income. When the company is thriving and its sales are growing quickly, its income is high, and it can afford to invest in new projects, pay its staff well, and manage its debts. But if the company makes a strategic decision that permanently reduces its sales potential—say, by cutting itself off from its biggest market—its income will be permanently lower. It will have less money coming in every single year from that point forward. This creates a structural problem.

This is precisely the situation the UK government found itself in after Brexit. The conclusion from economists and official bodies like the Office for Budget Responsibility (OBR) is that the UK economy is, and will remain, smaller than it would have been inside the EU—by a significant 4%. This isn't a one-off hit. It's a permanent reduction in the nation's economic horsepower. A smaller economy means less activity: fewer goods being sold, lower company profits, and suppressed wage growth. For HM Treasury, this translates directly into a smaller tax base. Every year, the government collects less in VAT, less in corporation tax, and less in income tax and National Insurance than it otherwise would have.

This creates a structural hole in the public finances. It's a permanent gap between the money the government needs to fund public services like the NHS, schools, and pensions, and the money it can realistically collect in taxes from a diminished economy. The numbers are stark. In the years following the Brexit vote, the UK saw a series of very large tax increases. While some of this was due to the costs of the pandemic, detailed analysis suggests a huge portion was needed simply to plug the Brexit-induced fiscal hole. Of the roughly £100 billion in tax rises implemented between 2019 and 2024, it is estimated that as much as £40 billion was necessary just to compensate for the economic damage—the lost growth and lost tax revenue—caused by leaving the EU. Put simply, a significant share of the recent tax burden on households and businesses is a direct invoice for the economic cost of Brexit.

Faced with this new reality, the government has had to change its approach. The first response has been to adopt a stricter fiscal framework. HM Treasury introduced new fiscal rules designed to ensure that the national debt begins to fall as a share of the economy's total size (GDP) within the next five years. This reflects a cold, hard truth: in a lower-growth world, you cannot afford to be as relaxed about borrowing. When an economy is growing quickly, it can more easily "grow out" of its debts. But when growth is weak, debt can quickly become unsustainable, spooking international investors and driving up the cost of borrowing for everyone. These tighter rules are an admission that the UK's fiscal room for maneuver has shrunk.

The second response has been an attempt to mitigate the damage through supply-side reforms—policies designed to make the UK a more competitive and attractive place to do business, in the hope of clawing back some of the lost potential. This has involved a wide-ranging review of thousands of EU laws that were retained on the UK statute book, looking for regulations that could be scrapped to reduce costs for businesses. More concretely, the government introduced a major tax incentive called "full expensing." This allows companies to deduct the full cost of new machinery and equipment from their taxable profits in the year they buy it. It's a powerful incentive designed to directly counteract the "investment strike" that Brexit caused, effectively giving businesses a large tax break for investing in their own productivity.

Ultimately, the UK's post-Brexit fiscal journey is a powerful real-world lesson in cause and effect. A major policy decision that permanently damages the supply side of the economy will inevitably show up on the national balance sheet. It forces policymakers into a series of difficult and often painful choices between raising taxes on citizens, cutting back on public services, or allowing the national debt to grow to more dangerous levels. The economic consequences of disintegration have become the defining fiscal challenge of a generation.

8.4 Monetary Policy in the Post-Brexit Environment

If the government's job has become harder, the task facing the Bank of England has become significantly more complex and fraught with danger. The Bank of England is the UK's economic firefighter. Its primary job is to keep inflation—the rate at which prices are rising—stable at a target of 2%. Its secondary job is to support economic growth and employment. In normal times, these two goals can often be pursued together. But Brexit has fundamentally altered the landscape, creating a situation where these two objectives are now much more likely to be in direct conflict.

The first tremor was felt immediately after the referendum result in June 2016. In the financial markets, the value of the British pound plummeted. For international investors, the vote signaled a riskier, less certain future for the UK, so they sold sterling. While this was a dramatic sign of lost confidence, the falling pound acted as a crucial, if painful, shock absorber for the economy. It instantly made all British exports cheaper for foreign buyers, providing a much-needed boost to UK companies selling abroad. However, it came at a price. A weaker pound meant that everything the UK buys from the rest of the world—from Spanish oranges to German car parts to the fuel in our petrol tanks—became more expensive. This surge in the cost of imports fed directly into higher prices in the shops, causing a bout of "imported inflation" that the Bank of England had to manage.

Beyond that initial shock, a more profound, long-term challenge has emerged. As we've established, Brexit has damaged the UK's supply side, reducing its potential growth rate. The economy's "speed limit" is now lower. This changes everything for the Bank of England. Before, the Bank could keep interest rates low to encourage spending and investment, confident that the economy had enough spare capacity to meet that extra demand without overheating. Now, that spare capacity has been reduced. The same amount of demand is much more likely to bump up against the economy's new, lower capacity limits, leading to shortages and driving up prices.

This creates a much more difficult trade-off for the central bank. The negative supply-side shock from Brexit makes the UK inherently more prone to inflation. Any disruption—a global energy price spike, a problem with a specific supply chain—is more likely to translate into sustained price rises because the economy is less flexible and efficient than it once was.

This leads to the central banker's worst nightmare: the "stagflationary" dilemma. Stagflation is the toxic combination of a stagnant economy (weak growth, rising unemployment) and high inflation. It puts the central bank in an impossible position. The standard medicine for high inflation is to raise interest rates. This makes borrowing more expensive, dampens demand, and cools the economy down. But if the economy is already weak and heading into a recession, raising interest rates is like throwing cold water on someone who is already freezing—it will only make the downturn worse, costing people their jobs.

This is the treacherous path the Bank of England now has to walk. Because of a structural policy decision to raise trade barriers, the Bank is now far more likely to face these stagflationary scenarios, where it is forced to choose between fighting inflation and protecting employment. By damaging the economy's efficiency, Brexit has effectively outsourced the most painful consequences to the monetary authority. The Bank of England is left to manage the macroeconomic fallout, armed only with tools that are ill-suited to fixing a problem that is fundamentally structural, not cyclical. It is a constant battle against inflationary pressures in an economy that has been made permanently less resilient.

Part III: Policy Challenges in Major Emerging Economies

Managing the Impossible Trinity: China's Balancing Act of Exchange Rates, Capital Flows, and Monetary Autonomy

Managing the Impossible Trinity: China's Enduring Balancing Act

In the grand theater of global economics, few dramas are as compelling or consequential as China's decades-long performance in managing the "Impossible Trinity." This core principle of international macroeconomics, also known as the policy trilemma, presents a stark choice to every nation: out of a fixed exchange rate, free international capital flows, and an independent monetary policy, you can only ever have two. A country can't have its cake and eat it too. The United States, for instance, chooses monetary independence and free capital flows, but in exchange, it lets the value of the dollar float freely on global markets. Hong Kong pegs its currency to the U.S. dollar and allows capital to move without restriction, but by doing so, it effectively outsources its monetary policy to the U.S. Federal Reserve.

For over four decades, China has charted a third, distinct path. It has resolutely prioritized the ability to set its own interest rates and control its own economic destiny (monetary autonomy) while simultaneously managing its currency's value to foster stability and export-driven growth (a managed exchange rate). The linchpin holding this seemingly impossible structure together is the deliberate sacrifice of the third vertex of the trinity: free capital flows. This strategic choice is not a temporary fix or a technical workaround; it is the very foundation of China's state-led economic model. This deep dive explores the theory behind the trilemma through the Chinese lens, traces the calculated evolution of its currency regime, and examines the intricate machinery of its capital controls and their profound implications for both China and the world.

The Trilemma's Strategic Calculus: Why Control is Non-Negotiable

The logic of the Impossible Trinity is both elegant and unforgiving. Imagine a world where China tried to have it all: a fixed exchange rate to the U.S. dollar, open capital borders, and its own independent monetary policy. What would happen? Suppose the People's Bank of China (PBOC) wanted to stimulate the domestic economy by lowering interest rates, making it cheaper for businesses to borrow. If U.S. interest rates were higher, and capital was free to move, a torrent of money would immediately flow out of China. Investors, both domestic and foreign, would sell their renminbi (RMB) to buy U.S. dollars and invest in higher-yielding American assets. This massive sell-off of the RMB would put immense downward pressure on its value, forcing the PBOC into a desperate battle to defend the fixed exchange rate. To do so, it would have to buy up RMB using its foreign currency reserves, and more importantly, it would be forced to raise its interest rates back up to match the U.S. level to stop the capital flight. In this scenario, its "independent" monetary policy would be rendered powerless, its decisions dictated not by domestic needs in Beijing, but by policy choices made in Washington D.C.

Faced with this stark reality, Chinese policymakers made a clear and consistent choice. For them, monetary autonomy has always been paramount. In a continental-sized economy with over 1.4 billion people, the government must have the tools to manage domestic credit, fight inflation, prevent asset bubbles, and stimulate growth on its own terms. Giving up that control would be unthinkable.

Simultaneously, a stable and predictable exchange rate has been a crucial instrument of industrial policy. It provided a bedrock of certainty for exporters, helping to turn China into the "world's factory." By preventing wild swings in the currency's value, the government could shield its industries from the volatile whims of global financial markets and maintain its competitive edge.

The solution to this puzzle—the way to have both domestic control and currency stability—was to build and maintain a formidable system of capital controls. This "Great Wall of capital" restricts the ability of individuals and companies to move large sums of money across the border for investment purposes. For policymakers in Beijing, the trilemma isn't a problem to be solved; it is a menu of strategic options. Their decision to forgo free capital flows is a conscious and enduring trade-off, a cornerstone that allows the state to insulate its economy from global financial shocks and steer its development with a firm hand. This choice reflects a deep-seated belief that for a developing nation of China's scale, financial stability and state control are more valuable than unfettered integration with the global financial system.

A Journey Through Time: The Calculated Evolution of China's Currency

China's exchange rate policy has never been static; it has been a dynamic tool, meticulously adapted to serve the nation's shifting economic strategies. This evolution can be seen as a series of distinct, deliberate phases.

In the early decades of the People's Republic, from 1949 until the reforms began in 1978, the RMB was pegged at a highly overvalued, officially determined rate. This was not a mistake; it was a core component of an inward-looking, import-substitution strategy. The goal was to build a heavy industrial base from scratch. An artificially strong RMB made it incredibly cheap to import the essential foreign machinery, technology, and factory equipment that China could not yet produce itself. The exchange rate was, in essence, a subsidy for industrialization.

The "reform and opening up" period, initiated in 1978, marked a gradual pivot towards the global economy. This transition was cautious and experimental. For years, China operated a confusing dual-track exchange rate system: an official rate and a more market-driven "swap rate" available at designated centers. This allowed the authorities to dip their toes in market waters without losing complete control, giving exporting enterprises access to foreign currency at a more realistic price. This messy but practical system paved the way for a major unification of the rates in 1994.

From 1994 to 2005, China adopted what became its most famous—and controversial—currency policy: a de facto peg to the U.S. dollar at a rate around 8.28 RMB to the dollar. This rate was widely seen as significantly undervalued, making Chinese goods extraordinarily cheap on the world market. It acted as a powerful rocket booster for China's export machine, fueling a historic economic boom and leading to the accumulation of the largest foreign exchange reserves in human history. However, this policy also generated immense friction with trading partners, particularly the United States, who accused China of currency manipulation to gain an unfair trade advantage.

Under mounting international pressure, China shifted gears in July 2005. It announced a move away from the hard dollar peg to a "managed float" regime, where the RMB's value would be set with reference to a basket of currencies of its major trading partners. In practice, this meant a slow, tightly controlled appreciation of the RMB. While more flexible in theory, the PBOC remained the ultimate authority, intervening heavily in currency markets to steer the RMB's path and prevent any movements it deemed too rapid or destabilizing. The surprise devaluation in 2015, which shocked global markets, was a stark reminder that "managed" was still the operative word. Looking ahead, the stated policy for 2025—to maintain a "basically stable" exchange rate while preventing "overshooting risks"—signals a continuation of this philosophy: stability above all, with carefully controlled flexibility. This history clearly shows the RMB is more than just money; it is a strategic lever of national power.

The Great Wall of Capital: Mechanisms and Global Consequences

To truly understand how China manages the trilemma, one must look beyond theory and examine the intricate architecture of its capital controls. These controls are not a single blunt instrument but a complex, multi-layered system designed to separate the flow of money for trade from the flow of money for investment.

At a high level, China operates a system that distinguishes between the "current account" and the "capital account." The current account, which covers the trade of goods and services, is now largely open. An exporter who sells goods to Europe can freely receive euros and convert them to RMB. The capital account, however, which governs cross-border investments like buying stocks, bonds, or real estate, remains tightly managed.

For individuals, this is most famously expressed in the annual quota that limits them to converting just $50,000 worth of RMB into foreign currency. For corporations, any significant outbound investment faces intense scrutiny from regulators to ensure it is strategically sound and not simply capital flight in disguise.

At the same time, China has not hermetically sealed its financial markets. Instead, it has built a series of carefully controlled channels to allow limited and monitored two-way flows. Programs like the Qualified Foreign Institutional Investor (QFII) and its RMB-denominated sibling (RQFII) act as gatekeepers, granting licensed foreign institutions specific quotas to invest in China's domestic stock and bond markets. More recently, the "Connect" schemes (Stock Connect and Bond Connect) have created direct linkages between the Hong Kong and mainland exchanges, allowing international investors to trade a selection of mainland assets through Hong Kong without needing a specific license or quota. These are not open floodgates; they are meticulously engineered sluices that allow the authorities to control the volume, speed, and direction of capital flows.

The global implications of this strategy are immense. For China, it has been an undeniable success in fostering stability. The capital controls largely insulated it from the devastating effects of the 1997 Asian Financial Crisis and the 2008 Global Financial Crisis. However, the system also creates distortions, such as trapping vast amounts of domestic savings within the country, which has arguably fueled real estate bubbles and the rise of a less-regulated "shadow banking" system.

For the rest of the world, China's choices are transformative. Its policy of intervening in currency markets to hold down the RMB's value has resulted in China becoming the largest foreign holder of U.S. Treasury bonds, a fact that gives it significant influence over global interest rates. The controlled nature of its capital account means that despite being the world's second-largest economy, its financial markets are still underweight in global investment portfolios, and the RMB's rôle as a global reserve currency remains limited. This presents China with its own forward-looking trilemma: to truly internationalize the RMB and challenge the U.S. dollar's dominance, it must eventually open its capital account. But doing so would mean giving up the very control that has been the bedrock of its economic stability for decades—a monumental risk that Beijing is not yet willing to take.

9.3 Capital Controls as the Lynchpin of the System

Imagine a master watchmaker building an incredibly complex and beautiful timepiece. Inside this watch, there are three main gears: one for setting the time independently (monetary policy), one for keeping the hands moving at a steady, predictable speed (a managed exchange rate), and one for easily opening the watch to let anyone tinker with the parts (free capital flows). The watchmaker, a craftsman of the highest order, knows a fundamental truth of horology: you can have any two of these gears working together perfectly, but you can never have all three.

For China, this is not just a theoretical puzzle; it is the daily reality of managing the world's second-largest economy. The People's Bank of China (PBOC) is that master watchmaker, and for decades, its choice has been unwavering. It insists on controlling the first two gears—the ability to set its own interest rates to manage its vast domestic economy and the power to keep its currency, the renminbi (RMB), stable and predictable. To make this delicate mechanism work, it had to deliberately sacrifice the third gear. That sacrifice, the decision to not allow money to flow freely across its borders for investment, is the lynchpin of its entire economic model. Capital controls are not just one tool among many; they are the central pin that holds the entire intricate system together. Without them, the whole machine would fly apart.

Let's bring this to life. As we look at the economic landscape in 2025, China's policymakers are focused on domestic challenges, particularly stabilizing a fragile property sector. To do this, they have signaled a "moderately loose monetary policy," which is simply a way of saying they want to lower interest rates to make it cheaper for businesses and individuals to borrow money, hoping to spark investment and growth. Now, picture what would happen if China had an open capital account, like the United States or the United Kingdom.

In this alternate reality, a Chinese investor sees that interest rates at home are being cut, meaning their bank deposits will earn very little. They look across the Pacific and see that the U.S. Federal Reserve is offering higher interest rates. The choice is simple. They would instantly sell their Chinese RMB, convert it into U.S. dollars, and move their money into American assets to earn a better return. This wouldn't be a trickle; it would be a flood. Millions of individuals and corporations, both Chinese and foreign, would make the same logical decision.

This massive sell-off of the RMB would put catastrophic downward pressure on its value. The PBOC would be trapped. It would be faced with a nightmare choice. It could either let the RMB's value plummet, which would abandon its cherished policy of exchange rate stability and create chaos for traders. Or, to stop the money from leaving, it would be forced to do the exact opposite of what it wanted to do for its domestic economy: it would have to raise interest rates back up to match the U.S., making its own monetary policy completely powerless. Its decisions would be dictated by Washington, not Beijing.

This is precisely the scenario that China's capital controls are designed to prevent. They act as a great, thick wall, separating China's domestic financial system from the powerful currents of global finance. While the wall isn't hermetically sealed, it is formidable. An ordinary Chinese citizen, for example, is famously limited to converting only $50,000 worth of currency per year for outbound use. For corporations wanting to make large overseas investments, the process involves intense scrutiny from regulators who must be convinced the deal is strategically vital for China, not just a clever way to move money out of the country. This system allows the PBOC to lower interest rates at home to support the economy, confident that this wall will prevent a disastrous exodus of capital.

However, this reliance on the wall—this lynchpin of stability—creates a profound and frustrating paradox for China's global ambitions. For years, a key strategic goal for Beijing has been to elevate the RMB into a true global currency, one that could stand alongside the U.S. dollar. The prize for achieving this is immense. The country that issues the world's primary reserve currency enjoys what has been called an "exorbitant privilege." It can borrow money more cheaply than anyone else and is insulated from certain types of financial crises.

But here is the catch: a currency cannot become a global reserve currency if it is kept behind a wall. For international banks, investors, and governments to truly embrace the RMB, they need absolute confidence that they can buy, hold, and sell RMB-denominated assets freely, whenever they want, in whatever quantity they want. They need deep, liquid, and, most importantly, open financial markets. China's capital controls make this impossible.

This presents Chinese policymakers with their own ultimate, high-stakes trilemma. They can have the domestic economic stability that their capital controls provide. Or they can have a globally dominant reserve currency, which would require tearing down those controls. For now, it is clear they cannot have both. The very policy that has been the bedrock of China's economic miracle and shielded it from financial storms is the same policy that shackles its currency's global potential. Every year, Beijing tinkers with the wall, opening small, carefully managed gates like the "Stock Connect" and "Bond Connect" programs, but it shows no sign of being willing to tear it down. The risk of losing control, of letting the unpredictable tides of global capital dictate its future, is simply a price it is not yet willing to pay.

9.4 Global Spillovers and Trade Tensions

If China's management of the Impossible Trinity is a complex machine operating within its own borders, its effects are anything but contained. The choices made in Beijing create powerful ripples that travel across the entire global economy, shaping trade relationships, creating financial dependencies, and often sparking intense political friction. This is not a contained experiment; the world is the laboratory, and we are all part of the results.

For much of the last quarter-century, the most visible and contentious of these spillovers has been the deliberate policy of holding down the value of the RMB. This wasn't a side effect; it was a central pillar of China's strategy to become the "world's factory." The logic is simple and brutally effective. By ensuring the RMB was cheap relative to other currencies like the U.S. dollar, China made its goods extraordinarily inexpensive for foreign buyers. A toy, a t-shirt, or a television that cost 100 RMB to make might have cost $12 on the international market, making it an almost irresistible bargain for consumers and importers in America and Europe. This policy acted like a powerful tailwind for Chinese exporters, fueling an unprecedented economic boom.

However, from the perspective of China's trading partners, this tailwind felt like a hurricane. Critics, especially in the United States, have long and loudly argued that this policy was a form of cheating—an unfair export subsidy that distorted global trade. They contended that it contributed directly to massive trade deficits and, more painfully, to the hollowing out of their own manufacturing industries. For a factory worker in a place like Ohio or Michigan, this was not an abstract economic debate. It meant their company was competing not just with a Chinese factory, but with the full might of the Chinese state, which was actively manipulating its currency to give its own producers a decisive price advantage. This led to the powerful accusation that China was "exporting unemployment," protecting jobs at home by effectively displacing them abroad.

The effect was not limited to the West. Other emerging economies in Asia found themselves in a difficult position. If they allowed their own currencies to appreciate naturally against the dollar, their goods would suddenly become more expensive and less competitive compared to China's. This created a chilling effect, deterring many from letting market forces work and pressuring them to also hold down their own currencies in a desperate bid to keep up.

The mechanics of this currency intervention created another profound global spillover: the creation of the world's largest stockpile of foreign exchange reserves. To keep the RMB from rising, the PBOC had to constantly step into the market, selling its own currency and buying up the foreign currency that was flooding in—primarily U.S. dollars. This process went on for years, resulting in China accumulating trillions of dollars in reserves. But China couldn't just let this cash sit in a vault; it had to be invested. The safest and most liquid place to park such vast sums of money was in U.S. Treasury securities, the debt issued by the American government.

This has created one of the most complex and fraught financial relationships in modern history. China became the largest foreign creditor to the United States, effectively lending enormous sums of money to the U.S. government, which helped keep American interest rates low. This interdependence is a source of both power and vulnerability for both sides. Some in the U.S. have expressed deep anxiety that China could one day use its massive holdings of Treasury bonds as an economic weapon—that it could threaten to sell them off, which would cause U.S. interest rates to spike and potentially trigger a financial crisis.

However, this power is severely constrained by a logic similar to that of nuclear deterrence: mutually assured destruction. If China were to dump its U.S. debt holdings, the ensuing panic would cause the value of the U.S. dollar to collapse. And since the vast majority of China's own savings are held in U.S. dollars, such an action would be an act of massive self-sabotage, wiping out the value of its own hard-earned reserves. It would be like burning down a house that you also happen to co-own.

As we move through 2025, this delicate balance continues to evolve. China is grappling with its own domestic economic headwinds, and the world watches its every move. Its choices on the exchange rate, its subtle adjustments to capital controls, and its domestic monetary policy will not stay within its borders. They will influence trade balances, shape global interest rates, and define the tone of international relations for years to come. China's trilemma is not just China's problem; it is a central, defining feature of our interconnected global economy.

Inflation Targeting in an Emerging Market Context: The Reserve Bank of India's Framework

10.1 The Pre-2016 Era: Grappling with the Dragon of High and Volatile Inflation

Imagine trying to plan your family's monthly budget when the price of groceries, gas, and electricity could jump unpredictably at any moment. This was the reality for hundreds of millions of Indians for years. Before 2016, India's economy was in a constant battle with a particularly stubborn beast: high and wildly fluctuating inflation. This wasn't just a number on a spreadsheet; it was a daily source of anxiety that eroded savings, punished the poor, and made long-term business investment feel like a gamble.

The journey through the 2000s and early 2010s was a true rollercoaster. The decade leading up to 2010 saw what started as a manageable inflation rate of 3.7% spiral into a dizzying peak of 12.1%. This created a climate of deep economic uncertainty. For a family living on a fixed income or a daily wage, a sudden surge in the price of onions or lentils wasn't an inconvenience—it was a crisis. It meant cutting back on other essentials, foregoing small joys, and seeing the value of their hard-earned money evaporate before their eyes.

But what was feeding this inflationary dragon? In many developed economies, high inflation is often a classic case of "too much money chasing too few goods," where strong consumer demand outstrips the economy's ability to produce. In India, however, the story was far more complex and deeply rooted in the very structure of its economy. The main culprit wasn't necessarily runaway demand but a series of relentless supply-side shocks.

Think of the Indian economy's dependence on two critical, and often volatile, elements: food and fuel. These two categories make up a huge portion of the average Indian household's spending, and therefore, they have an outsized influence on the headline inflation number, the Consumer Price Index (CPI).

First, there's the monsoon. For much of India's vast agricultural heartland, the annual monsoon isn't just a weather event; it's the lifeblood of the economy. A good monsoon means bountiful harvests, stable food prices, and prosperity for millions. A failed monsoon, on the other hand, means drought, crop failure, and an immediate, sharp spike in the cost of basic food items. This made food inflation incredibly difficult to predict or control. Compounding this were structural problems like inadequate infrastructure. Even in years with a good harvest, a lack of modern cold storage facilities and inefficient supply chains meant that a significant portion of produce would rot before it could ever reach the market, creating artificial scarcity and keeping prices high.

Then there's fuel. As a major importer of crude oil, India's economy is perpetually exposed to the whims of global energy markets. A geopolitical crisis in the Middle East or a decision by oil-producing nations to cut supply could instantly translate into higher petrol and diesel prices at home. This didn't just affect car owners; it raised the transportation costs for everything, from the food delivered to local markets to the raw materials shipped to factories, creating a ripple effect of price increases across the entire economy.

The Indian government's own policies sometimes added fuel to the fire. Large fiscal deficits, where the government spends more than it earns, often had to be financed in ways that could pump excess money into the system. Furthermore, policies like the Minimum Support Price (MSP) for crops, while designed to protect farmers' incomes, could also contribute to a higher baseline for food prices.

Perhaps the most dangerous aspect of this situation was how these supply-driven price shocks refused to remain contained. Economists initially hoped these spikes in food and fuel prices would be temporary "noise." But they weren't. They started to bleed into the wider economy. When people saw the cost of their daily meals and commute constantly rising, they naturally began to expect all prices to keep rising. They started demanding higher wages to keep up. Businesses, in turn, began raising the prices of their own goods and services to cover higher input and labor costs. This is what economists call "second-round effects," where a temporary shock becomes embedded in public expectations, creating a dangerous, self-fulfilling prophecy of persistent inflation. This was the true challenge for the Reserve Bank of India (RBI). Its primary tools, like adjusting interest rates, are designed to cool down or stimulate demand. They are like trying to use a thermostat to fix a leaky roof—the tool is simply not designed for the problem. Raising interest rates could do very little to solve a poor monsoon or lower global oil prices, but it could hurt economic growth by making it more expensive for businesses to borrow and invest. This left the RBI in an incredibly difficult position, trying to fight a multi-headed monster with one hand tied behind its back. The old approach, a "multiple indicator framework" where the central bank looked at many variables at once, lacked a clear, single goal, leading to confusion and undermining its credibility in the fight against inflation. It was clear that a new strategy was needed.

10.2 A New Dawn: Adopting the Flexible Inflation Targeting (FIT) Framework

Faced with the persistent challenge of volatile inflation that seemed to defy traditional policy responses, India's economic policymakers knew a fundamental change was necessary. The old way of doing things was no longer working. A consensus began to build, championed by a committee led by then-Deputy Governor Urjit Patel, that the RBI needed a clear, singular, and credible mandate. The answer was to formally adopt a modern monetary policy framework: Flexible Inflation Targeting (FIT). In August 2016, through a landmark amendment to the Reserve Bank of India Act, the country officially embarked on this new path.

This was more than just a technical adjustment; it was a philosophical shift. The amendment enshrined price stability as the primary, explicit objective of monetary policy. The logic was simple yet powerful: by anchoring inflation and making it low and predictable, you create a stable foundation upon which sustainable economic growth can be built. For the common person, this meant a future where the value of their savings wouldn't be mercilessly eroded year after year. For businesses, it meant being able to plan for the long term with confidence.

The architecture of the new framework was designed with clarity and accountability at its core. The Government of India, in consultation with the RBI, sets the inflation target. The goal was defined with precision: keep the headline Consumer Price Index (CPI) inflation at 4%. This target wasn't a rigid line in the sand. Recognizing the frequent supply shocks that buffet the Indian economy, the framework included a symmetric tolerance band of +/- 2 percentage points. This created an operational range of

2% to 6%. The goal was to keep inflation within this "comfort zone." This target is set for a five-year period, with the current mandate running until March 2026, providing a medium-term policy anchor.

One of the most significant institutional reforms was the creation of the six-member Monetary Policy Committee (MPC). This was a revolutionary step away from the old system where the RBI Governor held ultimate authority over interest rate decisions. The MPC was designed to be a more democratic and transparent body, bringing a diversity of views to the table. It consists of three internal members from the RBI—the Governor, a Deputy Governor, and another RBI official—and three external experts appointed by the government. These external members are typically eminent economists or academics chosen for their expertise. This blended structure fosters a healthy debate, combining the institutional knowledge of the central bank with fresh perspectives from the outside. Decisions on the crucial policy repo rate—the rate at which the RBI lends to commercial banks—are made by a majority vote, with each member having one vote and the Governor holding a casting vote in the event of a tie. The minutes of these meetings are published shortly after, providing unprecedented insight into the reasoning behind each member's decision.

This structure embodies a concept known as "constrained independence." The ultimate goal (the 4% inflation target) is set by the democratically elected government, ensuring that the monetary policy is aligned with the broader will of the people. However, the MPC is given complete operational independence to decide how to achieve that goal—whether to raise, lower, or hold interest rates.

Crucially, this independence comes with a strong accountability mechanism. The framework isn't a blank check. If the RBI fails to keep average inflation within the 2% to 6% band for three consecutive quarters, it is considered a breach of the mandate. In such a scenario, the central bank must submit a formal report to the government. This report has to explain in detail why the failure occurred, what remedial actions it plans to take to bring inflation back to target, and provide an estimated timeline for achieving this. This accountability clause is not just a formality; it builds public trust and puts pressure on the central bank to be transparent and proactive, ensuring it remains laser-focused on its primary objective. The "Flexible" in FIT is also key. It signals that the MPC, while prioritizing inflation, also has to be mindful of the growth objectives of the economy. It is not a robotic, single-minded pursuit of the inflation number at all costs. In times of a severe economic downturn, the framework gives the MPC the room to support growth, as long as it has a clear plan to guide inflation back to the target over the medium term. This pragmatic approach is tailor-made for the complexities of a large and diverse emerging market like India, balancing the critical need for price stability with the imperative of economic development.

10.3 Performance and Critiques of the FIT Regime: A Report Card with Nuance

If we were to give India's Flexible Inflation Targeting (FIT) framework a report card nearly a decade after its launch, the grades would be strong, but with some important teacher's notes in the margins. On the surface, the policy has been a resounding success. It took an economy plagued by a wild and unpredictable inflation beast and managed to put a durable leash on it. The change has been palpable, moving India towards a more stable and predictable macroeconomic environment.

Leading economists who have put the framework under the microscope, like Barry Eichengreen and his colleagues, have given it a firm thumbs-up. Their research paints a clear picture: since 2016, the monster of high inflation has been tamed. The numbers are not just lower on average, but they also don't swing around as wildly as they used to. This stability is worth its weight in gold. It means businesses can plan investments for the next five years without having to guess if their costs will suddenly double. It means families can save for their children's education with more confidence that their money will hold its value.

Perhaps the most crucial victory has been in the battle for hearts and minds. The framework has succeeded in "anchoring" inflation expectations. This is a fancy term for a simple, powerful idea: people are starting to believe that the Reserve Bank of India (RBI) will keep its promise to control prices. When the public trusts the central bank, it changes their behavior. They stop rushing to demand massive pay raises just to keep up with expected price hikes, and businesses become more cautious about passing on every small cost increase to consumers. This trust creates a virtuous cycle, making it easier for the RBI to do its job. Furthermore, the evidence suggests that when the Monetary Policy Committee (MPC) does adjust interest rates, those changes now ripple through the banking system and the broader economy more effectively than before. The policy levers are finally connected to the wheels.

However, no policy exists in a perfect, theoretical world. Scratch beneath the surface of this success, and you'll find a more complicated reality. Critics argue that while India has adopted the official rulebook of inflation targeting—the de jure framework—its actual behavior on the playing field—its de facto policy—doesn't always follow those rules. It's like a soccer team that says it's playing a certain formation but keeps moving players into different, unstated positions.

The first major point of contention is the exchange rate. A pure, textbook inflation-targeting regime requires letting the country's currency float freely, allowing its value to be determined by market forces. India, however, is deeply reluctant to do this. The RBI frequently and actively intervenes in the foreign exchange market, buying and selling U.S. dollars to manage the value of the rupee. Why? Because as a large emerging market, India is vulnerable to massive and volatile waves of international capital. A sudden surge of foreign investment can make the rupee too strong, hurting exporters. A sudden exit of that capital can cause the rupee to crash, importing inflation and creating financial instability. So, the RBI juggles, trying to prevent extreme volatility. But in doing so, it sometimes looks less like an inflation targeter and more like a country unofficially pegging its currency's value, which can complicate its primary mission.

The second critique points to a potential conflict of interest. The RBI wears two major hats: it's the nation's inflation fighter, but it's also the debt manager for the government. These two jobs can sometimes be at odds. As the inflation fighter, the RBI might need to raise interest rates sharply to cool down the economy. But as the government's banker, it knows that higher interest rates will make it much more expensive for the government to borrow the massive sums needed to fund everything from infrastructure projects to social welfare programs. This creates an inherent tension. Is the MPC's decision truly independent, or is it subconsciously influenced by the need to keep the government's borrowing bill manageable?

This brings us to the heart of the challenge for any large emerging economy: the "Impossible Trilemma." Economic theory tells us you can have any two of these three things: an independent monetary policy (like FIT), a stable exchange rate, and the free movement of capital across your borders. But you can't have all three. India has officially chosen monetary policy independence. But in practice, it's not willing to completely let go of exchange rate stability or fully absorb the shocks of free capital flows. It lives in a "messy middle," constantly trying to balance these competing objectives. This isn't a sign of failure, but a reflection of the complex, real-world trade-offs that don't fit neatly into an economic textbook. The FIT framework has been a great step forward, but its application in the real world is a masterclass in pragmatic compromise.

10.4 The 2026 Review: Fine-Tuning the Engine for the Road Ahead

As the March 2026 deadline for renewing the FIT framework approaches, the RBI is doing what any good engineer would: opening up the hood to see how the engine is running and what parts might need a tune-up for the next leg of the journey. This isn't a crisis-driven review; it's a proactive, healthy debate about the future of India's monetary policy. The RBI has invited experts, stakeholders, and the public to weigh in on some fundamental questions. Is the destination still the right one? And is the map we're using to get there still the best one available?

At the heart of this discussion are three critical components of the framework. First, the target itself. Should the MPC continue to chase the headline CPI inflation number, which includes every price from potatoes to petrol? Or should it switch its focus to a more stable "core inflation" measure that strips out the volatile food and fuel components? Second, is 4% still the magic number? Is it the optimal target that perfectly balances the need for price stability with the imperative of fostering economic growth? And third, is the +/- 2% tolerance band—the "guardrails" that create the 2% to 6% range—still the right width? Is it flexible enough for an economy that is constantly being hit by unpredictable supply shocks, like a bad monsoon or a global oil crisis?

One of the most concrete suggestions for reform focuses not on the target, but on the ruler used to measure it: the CPI basket itself. The way India calculates inflation is based on a representative basket of goods and services that the average household consumes. However, this basket was designed years ago. As incomes have risen and lifestyles have changed, the way people spend their money has evolved. The current CPI basket assigns a massive weight of 45.8% to food items. Many economists now believe this is outdated. In reality, food probably accounts for closer to 40% of household spending today and could fall to 30% within the next decade. Simply updating this weight to reflect modern consumption patterns would have a powerful effect. It would automatically make the headline inflation number less jumpy and less dominated by the unpredictable price of vegetables, making it a more reliable target for the RBI to pursue.

The debate that captures the central dilemma, however, is the "headline versus core" question. From a purely technical, central banker's perspective, targeting core inflation is incredibly appealing. It allows the MPC to "look through" the noise of food and fuel price spikes, which are driven by factors like weather and global politics that interest rates cannot influence. It would allow them to focus their tools on the underlying, demand-driven inflationary pressures in the economy—the part of inflation they can actually control. It would be a cleaner, more logical way to conduct monetary policy.

But here's the rub. Monetary policy isn't conducted in a laboratory; it's conducted in a society of over a billion people. For the vast majority of Indians, and especially for the poorest households, food and fuel aren't "noise"—they are the core of their daily existence. They are what determine whether a family eats well or has to cut back. Imagine a scenario where the RBI holds a press conference to celebrate hitting its 3% core inflation target, while the public is reeling from a 20% surge in the price of onions, cooking oil, and gas. The central bank would be seen as completely disconnected from the lived reality of the people it is meant to serve. This could shatter its public legitimacy and credibility, which are the very foundations of an effective inflation-targeting regime.

This dilemma is profound. It forces a choice between a policy target that is technically pure and one that is publicly relevant and accountable. It encapsulates the tightrope that the RBI must walk: balancing the science of economics with the art of public trust. As India heads towards 2026, the decisions it makes on these questions will not just fine-tune a policy framework; they will define the relationship between the country's most powerful economic institution and its people for years to come.

Part IV: When Policy Frameworks Come Under Stress

Post-Hyperinflation Fiscal Consolidation and Credibility: The Brazilian Experience

Post-Hyperinflation Fiscal Consolidation and Credibility: The Brazilian Experience

Brazil's economic story is a gripping saga of a nation caught in a devastating whirlwind of hyperinflation, a relentless battle for stability, and the eventual, hard-won prize of credibility. For Brazilians who lived through the 1980s and early 1990s, economics wasn't an abstract subject; it was a daily struggle for survival. The experience of multiple failed government plans, culminating in the celebrated success of the Plano Real in 1994, offers one of the most compelling real-world lessons in modern macroeconomics. It is a story about the corrosive power of inflation, the poison of lost government credibility, and the innovative genius required to restore faith in a nation's own currency and its future.

11.1 The History of Hyperinflation and Failed Stabilization Plans

Imagine waking up every morning knowing your money is worth less than when you went to sleep. Imagine rushing to the grocery store the moment you received your paycheck, because by the next day, the same bills in your pocket would buy significantly fewer groceries. This wasn't a hypothetical scenario; it was the lived reality for millions of Brazilians for over a decade. While the peak of this economic madness came in early 1990, with monthly inflation rates screaming past 70%—a figure that would equate to an almost unimaginable annual rate—this crisis was not a sudden storm. It was the final, violent rupture of a deep economic sickness that had been festering since the early 1980s.

The roots of the problem were buried in years of government policy. Brazil's persistent and large fiscal deficits were at the heart of the issue. The government was spending far more money than it was collecting in taxes. To cover this shortfall, it turned to the most convenient, and ultimately most destructive, solution: it ordered the central bank to print more money. This constant injection of new currency into the economy, without a corresponding increase in the production of goods and services, inevitably chased the same amount of products, driving their prices ever higher. The monetary policy of the time was not an independent force for stability; it was a servant to the government's spending habits.

Compounding this fundamental imbalance was a uniquely Brazilian phenomenon known as "inertial inflation." The economy had developed an institutionalized memory of rising prices. Decades of high inflation had led to the widespread adoption of indexation. Practically every corner of the economy was linked to the previous month's inflation rate. Wages, rents, contracts, and even taxes were automatically adjusted upwards based on official price indices. This created a powerful and vicious feedback loop. Last month's inflation automatically became a baseline for this month's price and wage increases, which in turn guaranteed high inflation for the next month. Inflation had a life of its own; it was a runaway train with no one at the controls, perpetually fueled by the expectation that it would continue. Breaking this cycle seemed nearly impossible.

Between 1985 and 1993, the Brazilian government launched a dizzying series of six major stabilization plans, each announced with great fanfare and hope. Each ultimately ended in failure, further eroding the government's already shattered credibility. The Plano Cruzado (1986) tried to stop the train by force. It introduced a new currency and imposed a sweeping price and wage freeze. Initially, it was wildly popular. Brazilians felt a sense of relief and even appointed themselves "price police," reporting stores that dared to raise prices. But the plan failed to address the core problem of government overspending. With prices frozen but money still being printed, consumer demand exploded, leading to massive shortages of goods, the emergence of black markets, and the eventual, chaotic collapse of the freeze. Inflation came roaring back with a vengeance.

Subsequent plans, like the Plano Bresser (1987) and the Plano Verão (Summer Plan, 1989), were essentially less ambitious reruns of the same idea: a heterodox shock involving freezes, but without the deep, painful, and politically difficult cuts in government spending needed to make it stick. Each failure made the public more cynical.

The most traumatic of these attempts was the Plano Collor in 1990, under the newly elected President Fernando Collor de Mello. It was economic shock therapy at its most brutal. In a stunning move, the government froze approximately 80% of all private financial assets for 18 months—from ordinary savings accounts to high-yield investments. The goal was to vaporize liquidity in the economy, killing demand and thereby strangling inflation. The economic logic was crude, and the human cost was catastrophic. Businesses were unable to make payroll, individuals were locked out of their life savings, and the economy plunged into a severe recession. While it did cause a temporary drop in inflation, the plan inflicted deep and lasting trauma on the population, utterly destroying what little trust remained in the government and the banking system. More importantly, the fundamental fiscal imbalance remained. As soon as the initial shock wore off, the inflationary engine, still fueled by government deficits, sputtered back to life. This parade of broken promises left Brazil in a desperate state, where the government's word meant nothing and its currency was a joke. It was from these ashes of failure and distrust that a new, radically different approach had to be born.

11.2 The Plano Real: A Successful Stabilization Case Study

By 1993, Brazil was at a breaking point. The cycle of failed plans had made it clear that another price freeze would be dead on arrival. The public simply would not believe it. A team of brilliant economists, assembled under then-Finance Minister Fernando Henrique Cardoso, knew they needed to do more than just stop inflation; they had to perform a kind of collective psychological surgery on the nation's economy. They had to restore credibility. Their solution, the Plano Real, remains one of the most innovative and successful stabilization programs ever conceived. Its success was not based on a single, shocking blow, but on a carefully sequenced, multi-stage strategy that brilliantly addressed both the fiscal and inertial roots of the crisis.

The cornerstone of the plan was a truly ingenious invention: the Unidade Real de Valor (URV), or the Real Unit of Value. The architects of the plan understood that the core of the inertial problem was the "unit of account"—the yardstick people used to measure value. The old currency, the cruzeiro real, was a broken yardstick, shrinking in value every single day. The URV was designed to be a new, stable yardstick, introduced while the old currency was still in circulation.

Here is how this remarkable mechanism worked. The URV was not cash; you couldn't go to a store and buy a loaf of bread with it. It was a virtual, parallel unit of account, and its value was pegged to the U.S. dollar. Every day, the Central Bank would announce the official exchange rate between the URV and the constantly depreciating cruzeiro real. As inflation chewed away at the cruzeiro, its value in URVs would fall accordingly. The genius of this was that it allowed the economy to gradually de-index itself from its own inflationary past.

The process was methodical. First, wages were converted into and quoted in URV. Then, government contracts and prices for public services followed. Soon, private businesses began pricing their goods and services in URV, even though customers were still paying for them in the old cruzeiros at the day's exchange rate. For the first time in years, people could look at prices and see stability. A bottle of soda that cost, say, 1 URV on Monday would still cost 1 URV on Friday. The price in cruzeiros would have skyrocketed, but in the new unit of account, it was perfectly stable. The URV was effectively a filter, allowing everyone to see through the fog of inflation and perceive the true, stable relative prices of things. It was a massive coordination device, getting the entire economy to "think" in a stable currency before that currency even existed.

This transitional phase lasted for about four months, giving society time to adapt. Then came "D-Day": July 1, 1994. The government introduced the new currency, the Real (BRL). The transition was seamless and elegant. The government simply declared that one Real was now equal to one URV. All of the prices and contracts that had already been converted to the URV were now denominated in the new Real. There was no shock, no freeze, and no trauma. The back of inertial inflation had been broken not by force, but by finesse.

Critically, this monetary magic trick was supported by a real commitment to fiscal responsibility. The plan's architects knew that the URV would be worthless if the government continued its old habit of printing money to pay its bills. To establish credibility, they implemented crucial fiscal reforms. They created an "Emergency Social Fund" which allowed the federal government to retain a portion of tax revenues that were previously, by constitutional mandate, automatically transferred to states and municipalities. This gave the central government newfound flexibility and control over the budget, allowing it to rein in spending.

The results were nothing short of miraculous. Annual inflation, which had been careening towards 5,000% in the 12 months leading up to the plan, plummeted to just 22% by the end of 1995. For the first time in a generation, Brazilians experienced price stability. The social impact was profound. The poor and working classes, who had no access to sophisticated financial instruments to protect their meager earnings, benefited the most. Their purchasing power soared, leading to a massive consumption boom and a dramatic reduction in poverty. The success of the Plano Real not only stabilized the economy; it restored a sense of national pride and proved that even the most entrenched hyperinflation could be defeated with intelligence, political will, and, above all, a credible plan that earns the people's trust.

11.3 The Social Impact of Hyperinflation and Stabilization

Hyperinflation is more than an economic phenomenon; it is a social disease that corrodes the very fabric of a nation. For over a decade in Brazil, this disease ran rampant, and its costs were paid most heavily by those least able to afford them. It wasn't just about rising numbers on a government report; it was a daily, grinding assault on human dignity and the ability to plan for a future. The experience left deep scars on the national psyche, and understanding its social impact is key to appreciating the monumental achievement of the stabilization that followed.

Imagine being a mother in São Paulo in 1993. Your husband, a factory worker, is paid his monthly salary in a bundle of cruzeiros reais. The moment he walks through the door, a frantic race against time begins. You don't deposit the money; there's no point. By tomorrow, it will be worth noticeably less. You immediately rush to the local supermercado, your shopping list a desperate calculation of what your family needs to survive the next few days. The prices on the shelves are not printed; they are written on chalkboards or displayed on digital counters that are updated multiple times a day. The price of milk might rise between the time you enter the store and the time you reach the checkout counter. This wasn't an exaggeration; it was reality. Your savings, if you were fortunate enough to have any, were a melting ice cube. This relentless depreciation of money is what economists call the "inflation tax." It is the cruelest and most regressive tax imaginable because it preys on those who live in the cash economy—the poor, the working class, and the elderly on fixed pensions. They lacked the access to the sophisticated bank accounts or financial instruments that the wealthy used to shield their assets, leaving them completely exposed.

The damage went far beyond the grocery store. The basic function of prices—to signal scarcity and value—was utterly destroyed. No one could make a rational business decision. A small business owner had no idea what to charge for their goods, because the cost of their raw materials was a moving target. Planning for the future became impossible. Why would anyone save for a child's education or a down payment on a house when the currency itself was a joke? It fostered a short-term, almost predatory, mindset focused on immediate survival. This uncertainty choked off investment, crippled production, and led to the economic stagnation of the 1980s, often called Brazil's "lost decade." Families were forced into desperate coping strategies. Teenagers who should have been in school were sent into the workforce to add another meager, and rapidly depreciating, income to the household. The informal economy boomed, not out of entrepreneurial spirit, but out of sheer necessity.

Then came the Plano Real in 1994, and with it, a profound and almost immediate social transformation. When inflation was finally slain, it was as if a crushing weight was lifted from the shoulders of the nation. The end of the inflation tax was the single greatest anti-poverty program Brazil had seen in a generation. Suddenly, that factory worker's salary held its value. The mother could now shop with a sense of calm, knowing the price of milk would be the same tomorrow, and the next week, and the next month. For the first time, families could budget. Their purchasing power, no longer being eroded daily, soared. This unleashed a massive consumption boom, particularly among the lower classes. They could finally afford basic appliances like refrigerators and televisions—items that had long been symbols of a middle-class life they could only dream of. The impact on poverty and inequality was immediate and dramatic. Millions were lifted out of poverty in the years immediately following the plan.

However, stabilization was not a panacea. It was a powerful medicine that cured the acute illness of hyperinflation, but it could not instantly heal the chronic, underlying conditions of Brazilian society. The country's deep-seated structural inequalities—rooted in centuries of history, regional disparities, and racial divides—remained. The newfound economic stability, in many ways, brought these issues into sharper focus. The favelas did not disappear. Access to quality education and healthcare was still vastly unequal. While the poor were no longer being punished by inflation, the gap between them and the rich remained one of the largest in the world. The legacy of instability left Brazil's social fabric fragile. Even today, with the horrors of hyperinflation a distant memory, the country remains vulnerable to macroeconomic shocks, and the fight for a more just and equitable society continues to be a long, arduous journey.

11.4 Contemporary Fiscal Challenges: Debt, Rigidity, and Reform in 2025

Three decades after the triumph of the Plano Real, Brazil in 2025 finds itself in a familiar, though less chaotic, struggle for fiscal credibility. The monster of hyperinflation has been caged, but the ghost of fiscal indiscipline still haunts the halls of government in Brasília. The challenges are no longer about stopping prices from spiraling by the hour, but about managing a vast and growing mountain of public debt, untangling a complex web of mandated spending, and forging the political consensus needed for deep, structural reform. The nation's long-term economic health depends on whether its leaders can address these issues with the same creativity and resolve shown by the architects of the 1994 plan.

The most glaring challenge is the sheer size of the public debt, which is steadily creeping towards 80% of the nation's Gross Domestic Product (GDP). This is a heavy burden for an emerging economy. This debt is not the result of a single crisis, but the slow accumulation of persistent primary deficits. In simple terms, for years the government has spent more on public services, salaries, and administration than it collects in taxes, even before accounting for interest payments. Compounding this problem is the Central Bank of Brazil's necessary fight against contemporary inflation. To keep prices under control, the bank has had to maintain high interest rates. While this monetary tightening is crucial for stability, it acts as a double-edged sword for government finances, dramatically increasing the cost of servicing the massive public debt. Each percentage point increase in the interest rate adds billions of reais to the bill the government must pay its creditors, creating a vicious cycle where the solution to one problem exacerbates another.

At the heart of Brazil's fiscal predicament lies a profound structural rigidity. The government's budget is not a flexible tool that can be easily adapted to changing economic conditions. Instead, it is a dense thicket of constitutional earmarks and indexed obligations. A huge portion of federal revenue is automatically directed to specific areas like health and education, and a significant percentage is transferred to states and municipalities. While these mandates serve important social goals, they leave the central government with very little discretionary spending to cut in times of need. Furthermore, many of the largest expenditures, particularly public sector pensions, are linked to the minimum wage. This means that whenever the minimum wage is increased to help the lowest-paid workers, it triggers an automatic and massive increase in pension payouts, regardless of the government's ability to pay for it. This institutionalized "stickiness" makes reallocating resources or making efficient spending adjustments nearly impossible without changing the constitution itself.

According to a landmark 2025 World Bank report, putting Brazil on a sustainable fiscal path requires a major adjustment, one that would be equivalent to achieving and maintaining a primary surplus of around 3% of GDP. Given that Brazil's tax burden is already high compared to other developing nations, the report concludes that the vast majority of this adjustment must come from cutting expenditures, not raising taxes. The proposed reforms are politically sensitive and strike at the core of vested interests. They include a comprehensive administrative overhaul to modernize public sector careers and control the wage bill, a move that is fiercely resisted by powerful public-sector unions. Another key, and highly controversial, proposal is to delink pension benefits from the minimum wage to break the cycle of automatic spending growth. Finally, the report suggests broadening the personal income tax base by closing loopholes and eliminating exemptions that disproportionately benefit the wealthiest Brazilians, ensuring a more progressive and equitable tax system.

The government's current framework, the New Fiscal Scheme, attempts to impose some discipline by setting limits on public spending growth. However, many analysts believe this cap may not be strong enough to stabilize the debt trajectory on its own. Without the deeper, more painful reforms, it may only slow the bleeding, not stop it. This creates a constant, difficult trade-off for policymakers. The need for fiscal consolidation is undeniable, but so is the need for public investment in infrastructure, education, and social programs to foster long-term growth and reduce inequality. Navigating this trade-off is the central economic challenge for Brazil in 2025. It is a battle for the country's future, a fight to ensure that the hard-won stability of the Plano Real becomes a permanent foundation for prosperity, not just a celebrated chapter in the history books.

The Evolution and Challenges of an Export-Oriented Growth Model: The South Korean Experience

12.1 The History of State-Led Industrial Policy and Export Promotion: Forging a Miracle from the Ashes

To understand South Korea's economic miracle, one must first picture its starting point. Imagine a landscape of ruin. In the early 1950s, following the devastating Korean War, the country was not just poor; it was a symbol of post-colonial, post-war despair. Its infrastructure was obliterated, its capital city, Seoul, was a sea of rubble, and its per capita income was less than that of many sub-Saharan African nations. The nation had few natural resources to speak of and a population struggling with basic survival. It was from this desolate ground that one of the most astonishing economic transformations in modern history would grow.

The initial attempts at recovery in the 1950s under President Syngman Rhee were faltering. The government tried an "import-substitution" strategy, aiming to replace foreign imports with domestically produced goods. It was a logical first step, but it was not enough. The domestic market was simply too small, and the industries remained inefficient, propped up by foreign aid without the competitive fire needed to truly innovate. The economy stagnated. The nation was adrift.

Everything changed with the military coup of 1961, which brought General Park Chung Hee to power. Park was a controversial figure, an authoritarian ruler who suppressed political dissent. Yet, he possessed an almost fanatical obsession with national development. He saw economic strength not just as a path to prosperity but as the ultimate guarantee of national security against the ever-present threat from North Korea. For Park, economic development was a form of warfare, and he would be its commanding general.

This new government swiftly abandoned the inward-looking policies of the past. It looked at South Korea's liabilities—a small domestic market, no natural resources—and decided to turn them into the foundation of a new strategy. If the home market was too small, they would sell to the world. If they had no resources to dig from the ground, they would cultivate their most valuable asset: their people. Thus began the great pivot to an export-oriented industrialization model, a high-stakes gamble that would redefine the nation's destiny.

This was not a free-market approach. Far from it. This was a "state-guided" or "developmental state" model, where the government was not a mere referee but the coach, captain, and chief strategist of "Team Korea." The government, under Park's firm hand, would actively intervene, picking industries, championing companies, and steering the entire national economy towards a single, overarching goal: exports.

At the heart of this strategy was the government's absolute control over the financial system. Upon taking power, Park's regime nationalized all major banks. This single move was the linchpin of his entire economic plan. Banks were no longer just financial intermediaries; they became the primary tool for implementing industrial policy. The government could direct capital wherever it wanted, acting like a national venture capitalist.

This gave rise to the system of "policy loans." The government would provide massive, low-interest loans to companies in targeted export sectors. The interest rates were often so low they were negative when accounting for inflation. This was practically free money, an enormous subsidy that gave Korean companies a powerful competitive edge. Access to this cheap credit was not a right; it was a privilege earned by meeting brutally demanding export quotas set by the government's powerful Economic Planning Board (EPB).

This system created an intense, symbiotic relationship between the state and a select group of private companies. The government needed corporate warriors to conquer global markets, and ambitious entrepreneurs needed the government's capital and support to grow. This partnership gave birth to the chaebol, the family-owned industrial conglomerates like Samsung, Hyundai, and LG (then called Lucky-Goldstar) that are now global household names.

In the 1960s, the government didn't just pick existing winners; it essentially created them. Park Chung Hee would personally meet with entrepreneurs like Lee Byung-chull of Samsung or Chung Ju-yung of Hyundai, giving them strategic directives and the financial fuel to achieve them. The deal was simple: the government would provide loans, tax breaks, protection from foreign competition at home, and help in securing foreign technology. In return, the chaebol had one primary duty: export, export, and export. Failure to meet export targets meant the flow of credit could be cut off, which was a corporate death sentence. Success meant even more support and the opportunity to expand into new, more ambitious industries.

The government's strategy was meticulously planned through a series of Five-Year Economic Development Plans, starting in 1962. The early plans focused on "vertical" policies, targeting specific light industries where Korea could leverage its large, disciplined, and low-cost workforce. The first export successes came from sectors like textiles, wigs, and simple plywood manufacturing. These were not glamorous industries, but they were crucial first steps on the industrial ladder. They brought in precious foreign currency and taught Korean firms the basics of mass production and international trade.

By the 1970s, confident from these early wins, Park Chung Hee made an even bolder move with the Heavy-Chemical Industry (HCI) Drive. This was a massive, state-mandated push into capital-intensive industries: steel, shipbuilding, automobiles, machinery, and electronics. It was an enormous gamble. These were sectors that development economists at the time believed a poor country like South Korea had no business entering.

The government's commitment was total. It established POSCO, a state-owned enterprise, to build a world-class integrated steel mill, a project the World Bank had refused to fund, deeming it unfeasible. It poured astronomical sums into Hyundai to create one of the world's largest shipyards from scratch. It nurtured Samsung's entry into the nascent electronics industry. The government protected these infant industries with high tariff walls, allowing the chaebol to sell products in the domestic market at a high profit, which could then be used to subsidize their lower-priced exports to break into fiercely competitive global markets.

Alongside these industry-specific "vertical" policies, the state also implemented "horizontal" policies designed to uplift the entire economy. Recognizing that human capital was its only real resource, the government invested massively in education. Literacy rates soared, and a generation of skilled and highly motivated engineers, managers, and workers was created. This educated workforce became a powerful engine for absorbing and improving upon foreign technology.

The government also established public research bodies, like the Korea Institute of Science and Technology (KIST), to act as a bridge for technology transfer. These institutes would license foreign technology and adapt it for use by Korean companies, helping them move from simple assembly to genuine innovation. Simultaneously, a colossal effort went into building the physical backbone of an export economy. Ports were dredged and expanded, the iconic Gyeongbu Expressway connecting Seoul to the southeastern industrial hub of Busan was built, and a reliable national power grid was established.

This entire system was a tightly managed, top-down affair. It was a relentless national project fueled by a sense of shared purpose and sacrifice. The "Miracle on the Han River" was not just a story of brilliant economic planning; it was also a story of immense human cost. To keep export prices competitive, labor unions were suppressed, and workers endured long hours for low pay in often harsh conditions. The nation's democratic development was put on hold in the name of economic progress.

Yet, the results were undeniable. From 1962 to the late 1980s, the South Korean economy grew at an average rate of over 8% per year. Exports skyrocketed from a mere $55 million in 1962 to over $60 billion by 1988. A nation that once exported wigs and sweaters was now exporting ships, cars, and semiconductors. It had, in the span of a single generation, clawed its way from the depths of poverty to the threshold of the developed world. The state-led, export-oriented model, driven by the powerful alliance between an interventionist government and the ambitious chaebol, had succeeded beyond anyone's wildest imagination. It laid the foundation for the modern, technologically advanced South Korea we know today, while also embedding deep structural challenges that the country would have to confront in the 21st century.

12.2 The Role of the Chaebol in Economic Development and Its Modern Challenges: Giants Forged in Fire

You cannot tell the story of South Korea's economic rise without talking about the chaebol. The word itself, meaning "wealthy clan," conjures images of immense power and sprawling influence. These are not just large companies; they are empires. Think of Samsung, Hyundai, LG, or SK. They are the colossal, family-owned conglomerates that were handpicked, nurtured, and unleashed by the state to be the shock troops of South Korea's export-oriented war on poverty. They are the architects of the "Miracle on the Han River," and today, they are the source of some of the nation's most profound economic and social anxieties. Their story is a dramatic tale of ambition, synergy, and the enduring challenge of a legacy that is both a blessing and a curse.

In the early days of Park Chung Hee's development push, the government faced a fundamental problem. How could a small, poor country create companies strong enough to take on the established industrial giants of Japan, America, and Europe? The answer was focus. Instead of spreading its limited resources thinly across thousands of small firms, the government decided to make concentrated bets on a few promising entrepreneurs. It would create "national champions." This was the genesis of the symbiotic, almost umbilical, relationship between the state and the chaebol.

The deal was straightforward and brutally effective. The government provided the chaebol with everything an aspiring industrialist could dream of. Through state-controlled banks, it channeled a torrent of "policy loans" at ridiculously low interest rates. It shielded their nascent domestic businesses from foreign competition with high tariff walls, allowing them to build a profitable base at home. It gave them tax incentives, direct subsidies, and access to scarce foreign currency needed to import machinery and technology. The state essentially acted as the ultimate venture capitalist, but one with the full power of a nation behind its investments.

In return, the chaebol had a single, non-negotiable mission: conquer global markets. They were given aggressive export targets, and their performance was relentlessly monitored by the government. Success was rewarded with more loans and the green light to enter even more lucrative industries. Failure meant being cut off from the flow of capital—a corporate death sentence. This high-pressure environment forged a generation of hyper-competitive, risk-taking entrepreneurs who led their companies with military-like discipline and a patriotic fervor.

This model allowed the chaebol to achieve something incredible: speed and scale. Chung Ju-yung of Hyundai, a man who started as a humble rice delivery boy, was given the state's backing to build the world's largest shipyard on an empty beach, even before he had any orders for ships. He famously convinced a skeptical foreign buyer by pulling out a 500-won banknote with a picture of a 16th-century Korean "turtle ship" on it, a symbol of the country's historic maritime prowess. Lee Byung-chull of Samsung made a monumental bet in the 1980s to enter the semiconductor industry, a move many thought was insane for a company that primarily made sugar and textiles. The government's support provided the safety net for such audacious gambles.

The chaebol grew into sprawling, octopus-like conglomerates, with tentacles in dozens of seemingly unrelated industries. Hyundai was not just in shipbuilding; it was in construction, automobiles, electronics, and finance. Samsung made everything from microchips and smartphones to life insurance and running theme parks. This diversification was a survival strategy. It allowed them to cross-subsidize ventures, using profits from a stable business to fund a risky new one. It also allowed them to quickly pivot into whatever new "target industry" the government's next Five-Year Plan had identified. They became the primary vehicles for executing the state's grand industrial vision, spearheading the nation's charge from poverty to prosperity.

However, the very features that made the chaebol such potent engines of growth in the 20th century have become formidable challenges in the 21st. The giants forged in the fire of industrialization now cast long, dark shadows over the modern Korean economy.

The most immediate problem is the creation of a deeply "dualistic" economic structure. The South Korean economy is often described as a landscape dominated by a few towering sequoias—the chaebol—surrounded by a struggling undergrowth of small and medium-sized enterprises (SMEs). For decades, the nation's resources, talent, and policy attention were lavished upon the giants, leaving the SMEs to wither. This has created a profoundly unlevel playing field. Chaebol can use their immense market power to squeeze suppliers, poach the best university graduates, and muscle out smaller competitors. This stifles innovation at the grassroots level, as potentially disruptive startups find it nearly impossible to compete for capital, talent, and market access against the entrenched conglomerates. The dream of being the "next Samsung" often dies in the shadow of Samsung itself.

Furthermore, the tight, collusive bond between big business and government has a dark side. What began as a strategic partnership for national development has, at times, devolved into cronyism and corruption. A recurring theme in modern South Korean politics is the scandal involving a chaebol leader and high-ranking government officials, leading to public outrage and calls for reform. This erodes trust in both the political and economic systems, fostering a public perception that the country is run by and for a small, unaccountable elite.

Perhaps the most dangerous modern challenge is systemic risk. The chaebol are not just big; they are "too big to fail." Their operations are so deeply woven into the fabric of the national economy—as major employers, exporters, investors, and borrowers—that the collapse of a single major chaebol could trigger a catastrophic economic meltdown. This is not a theoretical danger. The 1997 Asian Financial Crisis was a brutal wake-up call. It was triggered, in large part, by the reckless, debt-fueled expansion of the chaebol. Believing they had an implicit government guarantee, they borrowed massive sums to expand heedlessly, leaving them and the entire country horrifically exposed when the financial winds changed. The nation was forced to accept a humiliating bailout from the International Monetary Fund (IMF), a moment of profound national trauma.

Finally, the internal structure of the chaebol themselves presents a significant hurdle. They are famously hierarchical, opaque, and dominated by their founding families. Critical decisions are often made by an "emperor chairman," a patriarchal figure who wields almost absolute authority. While this top-down command structure was effective for executing large-scale industrial projects in the past, it is ill-suited for the fast-paced, decentralized innovation required in today's global economy. The rigid corporate culture can stifle creativity and make the giants slow to react to disruptive new technologies and business models.

Moreover, the issue of succession looms large. The transfer of control from the founding generation to their children and grandchildren is often a messy, controversial affair, sometimes marked by public family feuds and questionable backroom deals designed to circumvent inheritance taxes. This raises serious questions about corporate governance and whether the third and fourth-generation heirs, born into immense privilege, possess the same hunger, vision, and entrepreneurial grit as their pioneering grandfathers.

The chaebol are a paradox. They are South Korea's greatest economic achievement and its most pressing economic problem. They are a source of immense national pride and deep-seated public resentment. Reforming them is a delicate, perilous task. To dismantle them would be to kill the golden goose that powers much of the nation's export economy. Yet, to leave them as they are is to risk economic stagnation, widening inequality, and future crises. The ongoing struggle to redefine the role of these giants—to preserve their dynamism while curbing their excesses—is not just an economic debate; it is the central drama of South Korea's journey into the 21st century.

12.3 The Social and Economic Transformation from Developing to Advanced Economy: A Nation Reborn

To truly grasp the scale of South Korea's transformation is to witness a nation completely remake itself in the span of a single human lifetime. It is a story that defies conventional economic timelines, a compressed, high-speed evolution from utter destitution to dazzling modernity. The "Miracle on the Han River" was not just a line on a GDP chart; it was a fundamental rewriting of daily life, a collective upheaval that turned a landscape of rice paddies and thatched-roof huts into a skyline of glass-and-steel towers and a global hub of technology and culture.

Imagine South Korea in the early 1960s. The overwhelming scent in the air was that of earth and livestock. The vast majority of the population were farmers, their lives dictated by the ancient rhythms of planting and harvest. For most, the world was their small village. Their children were born in the same humble homes their ancestors had lived in, and they expected to be buried in the same nearby hills. Life was short, sustenance was precarious, and the future was a continuation of the past. This was the raw material—a poor, agrarian, and deeply traditional society—from which a global economic powerhouse would be forged.

The engine of this change was the government's all-out push for industrialization. This economic strategy triggered one of the most rapid and massive internal migrations in human history. A powerful current began to pull the population from the countryside towards the cities. It was a flood of human ambition. Millions of young men and women, seeing no future in the fields, packed their few belongings and boarded crowded trains and buses bound for Seoul, Busan, and the new industrial zones sprouting across the country. They were chasing a dream—not of great wealth, but of a steady factory job, a regular paycheck, and a life better than the one their parents had known.

This exodus fundamentally rewired the nation's social geography. Seoul, a city of ruins just a decade earlier, ballooned into a sprawling megacity. Hillsides on the urban fringe became crowded with hastily built shantytowns, known as "moon villages" (daldongne) because they were perched so high up they seemed closer to the moon. Life was tough. Families lived in cramped quarters, and the work was grueling. But these burgeoning cities were also cauldrons of energy and hope. For the first time, millions of people from different provinces were living and working together, their regional identities slowly melting into a new, shared identity as urban industrial workers, the foot soldiers of the nation's economic development. A new class of people, the "salaryman," was born, his life measured not by seasons, but by the punch clock and the monthly pay envelope.

This transformation was powered by a powerful, unwritten social compact—a set of shared values and sacrifices that became the human fuel for the economic miracle. The first and most important element of this compact was an almost superhuman capacity for hard work. Koreans of that generation worked with a desperate intensity. The official workweek was long, and overtime was practically universal. It was not uncommon for factories to run 24/7, and for workers to see their families only on rare holidays. This was not simply exploitation; it was widely accepted as a patriotic duty. The slogan "Let's live for tomorrow, not for today" echoed through society. People believed they were sacrificing their own comfort for the sake of their children and the future of their nation.

The second pillar of this compact was a national obsession with education. In a country with no significant natural resources, it became an article of faith that human capital was the only true path to prosperity. Education was seen as the great equalizer, the ultimate key to social mobility. Parents, including those who were illiterate themselves, would go to extraordinary lengths to ensure their children received the best possible education. They would sell their ancestral land, take on immense debt, and move their entire families just to get into a better school district. This "education fever" created a hyper-competitive academic environment, culminating in the brutally difficult annual college entrance exam, the Suneung, a single test that could determine a young person's entire future. This relentless focus on education produced a generation of highly skilled, literate, and disciplined engineers, scientists, and managers who became the brains of the new industrial economy.

The third element was an astonishingly high rate of savings. Driven by a deep-seated desire to invest in their children's education and a Confucian ethic of frugality, South Korean families saved a remarkable portion of their income. This personal thrift aggregated into a massive pool of national savings, which the government-controlled banks then channeled into the industrial chaebol. The sacrifice of individual consumption today was directly financing the construction of the factories, shipyards, and steel mills of tomorrow.

The results of this collective national project were staggering. The dry economic statistics—an average annual GDP growth of over 8% for three decades—fail to capture the lived reality of this change. It meant the near-total eradication of absolute poverty. It meant the arrival of electricity, clean running water, and modern sanitation in every corner of the country. It meant a nutritional revolution, as a diet once consisting of little more than rice and kimchi became rich with meat, fish, and dairy, causing the average height of an entire generation to increase. Life expectancy soared. A person born in 1960 could expect to live to be 52; a person born today can expect to live past 83.

Symbolic milestones marked the country's arrival on the world stage. Hosting the 1988 Seoul Olympics was a moment of immense national pride, a "coming out" party that showed the world a modern, dynamic, and confident Korea. Joining the OECD, the "club of rich nations," in 1996 was the official validation that South Korea had successfully made the leap from developing to advanced economy.

In the 21st century, the transformation has entered a new phase. Having conquered global markets for industrial goods like cars, ships, and semiconductors, South Korea has evolved into a cultural superpower. This phenomenon, known as Hallyu or the "Korean Wave," has seen the country's popular culture become one of its most influential exports. The infectious music of K-pop groups like BTS has topped charts around the globe. Korean television dramas and films, from the romantic comedies that sweep across Asia to globally acclaimed works like Parasite and Squid Game, are consumed by hundreds of millions. This is more than just entertainment; it is a powerful form of "soft power" that has also become a significant economic driver, boosting tourism, fashion, cosmetics, and food exports. A country once defined by war and poverty is now, for many young people around the world, defined by its style, creativity, and cultural cool.

The journey from a recipient of foreign aid to a global cultural and technological leader in a single generation is a story of immense sacrifice, relentless ambition, and profound change. It stands as one of the most remarkable development stories in human history—a powerful, though perhaps unrepeatable, testament to a nation's capacity for reinvention.

12.4 21st-Century Challenges: Competition, Demographics, and Slowing Growth: The Champion's Fatigue

For half a century, South Korea was the world's economic sprinter. It ran with a breathtaking, explosive speed that left the world in awe. Every decade brought a new lap of astonishing progress, moving from simple textiles to massive ships, then to sleek cars, and finally to the microscopic magic of semiconductors. The nation had a simple, powerful formula: make high-quality things and sell them to the world. This export-oriented strategy was the rocket fuel for the "Miracle on the Han River."

But no athlete can sprint forever. Today, the South Korean economy is like a champion marathon runner in the later stages of a grueling race. The explosive speed of the past is gone, replaced by a steady but slowing pace. The muscles ache, the breath is heavy, and the path ahead is no longer a straight, clear track. Instead, it is filled with formidable new obstacles: a ferocious new competitor running alongside, a shifting and treacherous geopolitical terrain, and a profound, internal fatigue that threatens to cripple the runner from within. The party of high-speed growth is over. The nation has successfully arrived at the destination of "advanced economy," only to find that this new place has its own set of profound and deeply complex problems.

The most immediate and jarring challenge comes from the east, in the form of a colossal shadow: China. For decades, the relationship was complementary. China provided a vast market for Korean goods and a low-cost manufacturing base, while South Korea provided the high-tech components and industrial know-how. Korea was the teacher; China was the eager student. But now, the student has not only graduated with honors but is building its own, bigger school. China is no longer just a customer or a factory floor; it has become a direct, head-to-head competitor in the very industries that South Korea once dominated.

This is not the old competition of cheap labor. This is a battle of technology, scale, and state-backed ambition. In shipbuilding, Chinese yards, backed by massive government subsidies, are churning out vessels at a scale and price that Korean shipbuilders find increasingly difficult to match. In steel and petrochemicals, Chinese industrial giants have flooded the global market, squeezing the profit margins of Korean stalwarts like POSCO.

But the most critical battleground is in electronics, the crown jewel of the Korean economy. For years, companies like Samsung and SK Hynix have been the undisputed kings of memory chips. Now, China is pouring hundreds of billions of dollars into its own semiconductor industry with the explicit national goal of achieving self-sufficiency and technological dominance. While they still lag in the most advanced technologies, they are catching up with terrifying speed. In other areas, like electric vehicle batteries and LCD/OLED displays, Chinese firms have already seized significant market share from their Korean rivals. The old playbook of being the world's high-tech workshop is under direct assault from a neighbor with nearly limitless resources and an iron will to win.

Compounding this competitive pressure is a global landscape that is growing colder and more hostile to the free trade that South Korea depends on for its very survival. The nation's economy is a classic "export powerhouse," meaning it is exquisitely sensitive to the health and openness of the global trading system. When the world is buying, Korea thrives. When trade routes are disrupted, or walls go up, Korea catches a cold.

In recent years, the rise of trade protectionism, exemplified by policies like the United States' "America First" approach and the broader trend of nations prioritizing domestic industries, has created a storm of uncertainty. Suddenly, the reliable markets that Korean companies spent decades cultivating are subject to unpredictable tariffs, regulations, and political whims. The escalating geopolitical rivalry between the United States and China has placed South Korea in an almost impossible position. It is, as the old Korean proverb says, a "shrimp among whales." It relies on the U.S. for its national security and as a key technological partner, but its economic lifeblood flows through China, which remains its single largest trading partner. Being forced to choose sides in a tech war or a trade dispute is a nightmare scenario, one that threatens to sever the critical supply chains that underpin its entire industrial structure.

Yet, as menacing as these external threats are, the most dangerous challenge—the one that keeps economists and policymakers up at night—is a slow-burning crisis from within. It is a silent, creeping threat that is far harder to fight than a foreign competitor or a trade tariff. It is the demographic time bomb.

South Korea has the unfortunate distinction of holding the world's lowest birth rate. For years, the number has been hovering far below the "replacement level" of 2.1 children per woman needed to maintain a stable population. In fact, it has fallen below 0.8, a number that demographers consider catastrophic. The reasons for this are deeply rooted in the pressures of modern Korean society: the astronomical cost of housing and private education, a notoriously grueling work culture that makes raising a family difficult, and a persistent gender gap that places a disproportionate burden of childcare on women.

The consequences of this demographic cliff are just beginning to be felt, and they are terrifying. The most immediate impact is a shrinking workforce. Every year, there are fewer young people entering the job market to replace those who are retiring. Who will work in the vast factories and high-tech labs? Who will drive the innovation and consumption that an economy needs to grow? This demographic drag is putting a powerful brake on the country's potential growth.

At the same time, the population is aging faster than any other in the developed world. The same generation that powered the "Miracle on the Han River" with their sweat and sacrifice is now entering old age. This creates a looming fiscal crisis. A smaller base of working-age taxpayers must somehow support a rapidly expanding population of retirees who need pensions, healthcare, and social services. The strain on the national budget and healthcare system will be immense. You can already see the early signs: elementary schools in rural areas are closing for lack of children, universities are struggling to fill quotas, and the military is worrying about future recruitment.

This perfect storm of intense foreign competition, global uncertainty, and a domestic demographic crisis is reflected in the country's dimming economic outlook. The high-octane growth of 8-10% is a distant memory. Today, organizations like the Korea Development Institute and the IMF are forecasting growth rates hovering around 2% for 2025, and many fear that even this may be optimistic.

There is a growing, uneasy consensus that the nation has entered a prolonged era of low growth, a "new normal" that it is psychologically and structurally unprepared for.

The fundamental challenge for South Korea in the 21st century is to accept that the old formula for success is no longer sufficient. The model that lifted it out of poverty—a state-led, export-focused, chaebol-driven dash for growth at all costs—is now showing its age and its limits. Navigating this new era will require a profound and difficult reinvention. It will mean fostering a more innovative and dynamic ecosystem of small and medium-sized businesses to complement the chaebol. It will mean tackling the deep-seated social issues that are driving its demographic decline. And it will mean shifting from a strategy based on simply growing bigger and faster to one focused on building a more resilient, equitable, and sustainable economy. The champion sprinter must now learn the art of the long, strategic marathon.

The Sovereign Debt Cycle: Argentina's Recurring Crises, Restructuring, and Reform

The Sovereign Debt Cycle: Argentina's Recurring Crises, Restructuring, and Reform

Argentina's economic story is a dramatic one, marked by incredible promise and devastating setbacks. It's a tale of a nation seemingly trapped in a powerful cycle, a recurring loop of borrowing, booming, and then busting. This isn't just about numbers on a spreadsheet; it's about the very real human cost of financial instability, a cycle that has shaped the lives of generations. From the historic default of 2001 to the radical economic experiment currently underway, Argentina serves as a stark and fascinating lesson in the world of sovereign debt. We will journey through this history, exploring the deep roots of its problems, the spectacular collapses, the brutal fights with creditors, and the latest audacious attempt to finally break the pattern.

The Deep Roots of a Recurring Problem

Argentina's struggle with debt isn't a recent phenomenon. It's a story with roots stretching back over a century. In the early 20th century, Argentina was one of the wealthiest nations on Earth, its prosperity built on vast agricultural exports. But this golden age masked underlying weaknesses. Political instability became a constant feature, with military coups and dramatic shifts in policy creating a volatile environment for long-term economic planning.

This instability fostered a culture of short-term thinking. Governments of all stripes found it easier to spend more than they collected in taxes, covering the difference by printing money or borrowing from abroad. When commodity prices were high and foreign capital was cheap, this system worked. The country would experience a boom, fueled by debt. But when the global winds changed—a dip in soy prices, a rise in U.S. interest rates—the flow of money would reverse.

Suddenly, the debt, often denominated in U.S. dollars, became impossible to repay with a devaluing peso. This is the core of the cycle. A boom built on foreign borrowing created a vulnerability that would inevitably lead to a bust, followed by default, painful austerity, and a period of being locked out of international markets. Then, after a few years, the memory would fade, a new government would come in, and the cycle would begin anew. This wasn't just bad luck; it was a deeply ingrained pattern of fiscal indiscipline and a reliance on external financing that set the stage for the massive crises to come.

The Anatomy of a Meltdown: The 2001 Collapse

The year 2001 is burned into the collective memory of Argentina. It was the year everything fell apart in the most spectacular fashion. The crisis was the culmination of a decade-long policy known as the Convertibility Plan. In an attempt to slay the beast of hyperinflation, the government in 1991 had pegged the Argentine peso to the U.S. dollar at a one-to-one rate. It was a monetary straitjacket: for every peso in circulation, there had to be a U.S. dollar in the central bank.

For a while, it worked wonders. Inflation vanished, and the economy stabilized. But the peg became a trap. As the U.S. dollar strengthened globally, so did the peso, making

Argentine exports incredibly expensive and uncompetitive. The economy plunged into a brutal four-year recession. The government, unable to devalue its currency, responded with deep spending cuts and borrowing, digging the debt hole ever deeper.

By late 2001, the breaking point was reached. Confidence evaporated. People rushed to pull their dollars out of the banks, fearing the peg would collapse. In a desperate move, the government imposed the infamous "corralito," a freezing of all bank accounts. This lit the fuse. Millions of ordinary Argentines were cut off from their life savings. Spontaneous, leaderless protests erupted across the country. People flooded the streets, banging pots and pans, a sound that became the soundtrack of the collapse. The social fabric tore apart. The political system imploded, cycling through five presidents in less than two weeks. Finally, on Christmas Eve of 2001, the government declared default on $93 billion of its debt. It was the largest sovereign default in history, a national trauma that would shape the country for decades.

The Vultures Circle: A Decade of Legal Warfare

The aftermath of the 2001 default was not a clean break. It was the beginning of a long and bitter war fought not on a battlefield, but in a New York courtroom. After the default, Argentina adopted a hardline stance. In 2005, President Néstor Kirchner's government made a stark offer to its creditors: accept new bonds worth roughly 30 cents for every dollar of original debt, or get nothing. With few other options, owners of about 76% of the defaulted bonds accepted the deal. Another swap in 2010 brought the total acceptance rate to over 92%.

But a small, determined group of creditors refused. These were the "holdouts," pejoratively nicknamed "vulture funds." Their strategy was different. Led by hedge funds like Elliott Management, they had bought Argentine bonds for pennies on the dollar on the secondary market after the default. Their goal wasn't to negotiate; it was to sue for 100% of the original face value plus interest.

Their legal weapon was a clause in the bond contracts called pari passu, a Latin phrase meaning "on equal footing." They argued this meant Argentina could not legally pay the holders of its new, restructured bonds unless it also paid them—the holdouts—in full. For years, the argument went nowhere. But then, U.S. District Judge Thomas Griesa sided with the holdouts. In a world-shaking ruling, he blocked Argentina from making payments to its restructured bondholders unless it paid the holdouts simultaneously. This created an impossible situation and, in 2014, pushed Argentina into a second, "technical" default. The country was once again a pariah in the financial world, held hostage by a small group of determined litigants.

A False Dawn: The Macri Years and Another IMF Bailout

In late 2015, a change in government seemed to promise a new beginning. President Mauricio Macri, a pro-business leader, vowed to end Argentina's economic isolation. One of his first acts was to settle the long-running legal battle with the holdout creditors. After 15 years, the fight was over. The settlement, which cost Argentina nearly $10 billion, was expensive, but it opened the door for the country to return to the international capital markets.

And return it did. Investors, hungry for high yields in a world of low interest rates, were eager to lend. Argentina issued billions in new debt, including a now-infamous 100-year bond. It felt like a vote of confidence, a sign that the cycle was finally broken. The government used the borrowed funds to finance its budget deficit, hoping that market-friendly reforms would spur investment and growth, eventually closing the fiscal gap.

But the old problems lingered. Stubbornly high inflation continued to erode confidence. A historic drought crippled the agricultural sector, the country's main source of export dollars. In 2018, the global financial tide turned. As the U.S. Federal Reserve raised interest rates, the flow of cheap money into emerging markets like Argentina stopped and then violently reversed. The peso's value plummeted. Facing another full-blown crisis, Macri turned to the last resort: the International Monetary Fund (IMF). Argentina secured the largest loan in the IMF's history, a staggering $57 billion. Yet even this historic bailout couldn't stabilize the economy. The debt burden was simply too large, the recession too deep. The familiar cycle had repeated itself with terrifying speed. By 2020, Argentina had defaulted yet again.

The Chainsaw and the Shock Therapy: Milei's Radical Experiment

By the time Javier Milei, a radical libertarian economist, took office in December 2023, Argentina was on the brink of hyperinflation. Prices were rising at an annualized rate of over 200%. The central bank was out of foreign reserves. The economy was a tangled mess of price controls, import restrictions, and multiple exchange rates. The situation felt desperate, demanding a drastic response. Milei promised exactly that with his program of "shock therapy."

His approach was unlike anything tried before. He nicknamed his plan the "chainsaw" for its focus on ruthlessly cutting state spending. He immediately slashed the number of government ministries in half. He announced massive cuts to energy and transport subsidies that had kept prices artificially low for years. He devalued the official exchange rate of the peso by over 50% in a single day to bring it closer to its real value. He put a hard stop on the central bank printing money to finance the government, the root cause of Argentina's chronic inflation.

The initial impact has been brutal, a form of economic chemotherapy. The devaluation and subsidy cuts caused an immediate spike in prices, pushing monthly inflation to over 25% in December 2023. The economy has been thrown into a deep recession as public works projects have been frozen and consumer purchasing power has collapsed. Poverty levels have soared. Yet, at the same time, there are signs that the shock is working as intended. The government achieved a monthly fiscal surplus in early 2024 for the first time in over a decade. Monthly inflation has begun to cool significantly. The central bank is slowly rebuilding its reserves. Argentina is now a live, real-time experiment. The question on everyone's mind is whether this painful, radical surgery can finally cure the patient and break the cycle, or if it is simply too much for the Argentine people to bear.

13.2 The IMF-Argentina Saga: A Symbiotic and Contentious Relationship

To understand Argentina's economic soul, one must understand its relationship with the International Monetary Fund. It is not merely a relationship between a debtor nation and a global lender. It is a saga. It's a long, tangled, and deeply emotional drama that has spanned nearly seventy years, filled with epic bailouts, bitter betrayals, defiant gestures of independence, and desperate returns. This is the story of the IMF's most challenging client and the nation that has become its single largest debtor. It is a push-and-pull, a symbiotic dance where both partners seem unable to live with each other, yet find themselves perpetually unable to live without each other.

The history is staggering. Since joining the Fund in 1956, Argentina has signed on to 23 separate arrangements. That number alone tells a powerful story. It speaks of a nation in a state of near-permanent economic crisis, repeatedly turning to the world's financial firefighter for help. Each agreement came with a promise of stability and a thicket of conditions—demands for spending cuts, tighter monetary policy, and structural reforms. And nearly every agreement has ended in failure, collapsing under the weight of political resistance, economic miscalculation, or a simple inability to escape the gravitational pull of Argentina's dysfunctional economic patterns. This cycle of rescue and collapse has left deep scars on the national psyche, making the very letters "IMF" (or FMI in Spanish) a trigger for passionate debate and public anger.

The Original Sin: The Collapse of 2001

While the relationship had been rocky for decades, the crisis of 2001 transformed it into something far more toxic. In the years leading up to the historic default, Argentina was the IMF's star pupil. The country's currency was pegged to the dollar, a policy the Fund had initially supported as a powerful tool against hyperinflation. The IMF poured billions into the country to support this system. But as the economy tipped into a deep recession and the currency peg became an economic straitjacket, the IMF's position began to shift.

In late 2001, with social unrest brewing and the country's finances in freefall, the IMF made a fateful decision. It refused to release the next tranche of its loan, concluding that Argentina's debt was unsustainable and its political leaders were unable to make the necessary cuts. For many Argentines, this was the ultimate act of betrayal. They saw it as the IMF pulling the plug on a patient it had helped put on life support in the first place. The decision precipitated the final, catastrophic collapse. The default, the bank freezes, and the political chaos that followed were all laid at the Fund's doorstep. The IMF was no longer seen as a flawed partner, but as a foreign villain that had enforced painful austerity and then abandoned the country in its darkest hour. This memory would poison the relationship for a generation.

The Breakup: "Nunca Más al FMI"

The years following the default were defined by a powerful act of defiance. Néstor Kirchner, who came to power in 2003, channeled the nation's anger. He governed on a platform of heterodox economics and blistering nationalism, casting the IMF and foreign creditors as predatory actors who had crippled the nation. His government's policy was to grow its way out of the crisis, not to submit to externally imposed austerity.

The ultimate expression of this defiance came in 2006. In a move that stunned the financial world, Kirchner's government took a chunk of the central bank's growing reserves and paid off Argentina's entire outstanding debt to the IMF—all $9.5 billion of it—in a single payment. The message was unmistakable: We are free. The slogan became "Nunca más al FMI"—Never again to the IMF. It was a declaration of economic sovereignty, a moment of profound national catharsis. For over a decade, Argentina went its own way. It was locked out of international capital markets, but it didn't care. It financed its spending through commodity export revenues and by printing money, enjoying a period of high growth while proudly keeping the IMF at arm's length. The painful memories of austerity and collapse faded, replaced by a sense of populist pride.

The Reluctant Reunion: Macri's Record-Breaking Gamble

But the old ghosts of Argentine economics never truly disappear. The populist policies of the Kirchner era, while popular, eventually led to the familiar problems: soaring inflation, a distorted exchange rate, and dwindling central bank reserves. By 2015, the country was ready for a change. The election of the pro-business Mauricio Macri seemed to signal a turning point, a return to economic orthodoxy and a reintegration with the global financial system.

Macri's government settled with the holdout creditors, reopened access to capital markets, and began dismantling the complex web of economic controls. But his gradualist approach failed to tame inflation or close the fiscal deficit. In 2018, as a global shift in financial conditions sent the peso into a nosedive, Macri found himself facing a terrible choice. He could either let the economy collapse or swallow his pride and go back to the one institution Argentines loved to hate.

He chose the latter. The result was the largest loan package in the history of the International Monetary Fund: a staggering $57 billion standby arrangement. The IMF, for its part, was eager to support a market-friendly government in a major emerging economy. It seemed like a chance to finally get the relationship right. But it was a spectacular failure. The money poured in, but confidence never returned. The economy continued to sink, inflation soared, and the debt burden became even more crushing. The program was so unsuccessful that the IMF later conducted a rare and candid internal review, admitting its own projections had been overly optimistic and that the program had failed to achieve its objectives. The cycle had turned once more. The historic loan had only served to saddle Argentina with an even bigger IMF debt, deepening the sense of entrapment and resentment.

A New Chapter or the Same Old Story? Milei and the IMF

This long and painful history set the stage for the dramatic events of today. When Javier Milei took office, the country was again on the ropes, with the failed 2018 IMF program hanging over it like a storm cloud. But Milei was a different kind of leader. A radical libertarian, he wasn't interested in the traditional dance of negotiating gradual reforms with the IMF. His platform was the very "shock therapy" that the IMF itself had often been accused of prescribing, but taken to an unimaginable extreme.

The dynamic between Milei and the IMF is perhaps the most fascinating chapter in this saga yet. The Fund finds itself in the strange position of backing a leader who is implementing a fiscal adjustment far more severe than anything it would have dared to propose itself. The new $20 billion program, secured in April 2025, is a bet on Milei's "chainsaw" plan. The IMF, having failed with both orthodox and gradualist approaches in the past, seems to have decided that perhaps only a radical, internally-driven shock can break Argentina's deep-seated patterns of overspending and money printing.

This alliance is fraught with risk for both sides. For the IMF, it is a high-stakes gamble on a volatile and unconventional leader. If Milei's program succeeds, the Fund can claim it supported a historic turnaround. If it fails, plunging the country into social chaos, the IMF will be accused of enabling a catastrophic experiment. For Argentina, the relationship remains as polarizing as ever. Milei's supporters see the IMF's backing as a stamp of approval, a sign that the world finally sees a government serious about reform. His opponents see it as the latest chapter in a long history of surrendering national sovereignty, a foreign seal of approval for a program inflicting immense pain on the poorest Argentines. The saga continues, a testament to a deeply intertwined, dysfunctional, and inescapable relationship at the heart of Argentina's perennial struggle for stability.

13.3 The Social Consequences of Economic Crisis and Austerity

The story of Argentina's debt is often told through the language of finance: billions of dollars, interest rates, fiscal deficits, and bond yields. But to truly understand the country's recurring tragedy, we must look past the spreadsheets and into the streets, homes, and soup kitchens. The sovereign debt cycle is not an abstract economic phenomenon. It is a relentless, punishing force that has inflicted a profound and lasting human cost on generations of Argentines. Each boom-and-bust cycle, each default, and each subsequent wave of austerity leaves behind a devastating wake of shattered lives, deepened poverty, and a fraying social fabric. This is the story of the "social debt"—the uncounted liabilities of lost potential, eroded health, and stolen futures that are the true price of financial instability.

The numbers themselves are staggering, painting a bleak picture of a society pushed to its limits. The collapse of 2001-2002 was a national trauma that saw the economy shrink by an almost unbelievable 20%. Unemployment skyrocketed past 25%. The poverty rate exploded, engulfing more than half the population. People who had spent their lives firmly in the middle class suddenly found themselves standing in line for a box of food, their savings wiped out overnight by devaluation and bank freezes. The recent crisis, culminating in the "shock therapy" of late 2023, has brought a chilling sense of déjà vu. By the early months of 2024, the poverty rate had surged to a shocking 55.5%, meaning more than one in every two Argentines could not afford a basic basket of goods and services. Even more harrowing, the extreme poverty rate—the measure of those who cannot even afford enough food—hit 17.5%. These are not just statistics; they are millions of individual stories of hardship and quiet desperation.

The Price on the Plate: Hunger in the Breadbasket of the World

Perhaps the most cruel irony of Argentina's situation is the prevalence of hunger in a country famous for its agricultural bounty. Argentina is one of the world's great breadbaskets, a land of sprawling pampas that produce enough food to feed a population many times its size. Yet, for a growing portion of its own people, a nutritious meal has become a luxury. The cycle of crisis directly attacks the dinner table. Soaring inflation, especially on food items, mercilessly erodes the purchasing power of the peso. A salary that could feed a family at the beginning of the month is often insufficient by the end of it.

The impact on children is a silent emergency. Studies from the current crisis reveal a heartbreaking reality: 57% of all children and adolescents are living in monetary poverty. This translates into millions of young lives shaped by scarcity. In neighborhoods across the country, community-run soup kitchens, or comedores, have seen demand explode. These are often run by volunteer mothers, who pool their meager resources to cook giant pots of stew or pasta to ensure the neighborhood children get at least one meal a day. They speak of seeing more and more new faces, many from families who never imagined they would need such help. They tell stories of children arriving who haven't eaten since the previous day's meal at the same soup kitchen. This is the face of social debt: a generation of children whose physical and cognitive development is being stunted by malnutrition, a loss that will handicap the nation's future productivity for decades to come.

A System in Collapse: The Erosion of Health and Education

Beyond the immediate crisis of hunger, the austerity that inevitably follows a financial collapse systematically dismantles the pillars of a healthy society: public health and education. Fiscal adjustment programs demand cuts, and these essential services are often the first to feel the squeeze. For ordinary Argentines, this means a healthcare system that is increasingly unable to care for them.

Hospitals run out of basic supplies. The cost of medicine, often priced in dollars, skyrockets beyond the reach of the average person. A recent report highlighted a 20% drop in the purchase of medications for chronic illnesses like diabetes and heart conditions. This is a terrifying statistic. It means that millions are being forced to ration their insulin, skip their blood pressure pills, or simply go without, hoping for the best. It's a gamble with their lives, forced upon them by economic circumstance. Retirees on pensions decimated by inflation are particularly vulnerable, often having to choose between buying medicine and buying food.

The public education system, once a source of immense national pride, suffers a similar decline. School buildings fall into disrepair. Teachers, whose salaries are ravaged by inflation, are often forced to work multiple jobs, their focus and energy drained. Families struggling to survive have less capacity to support their children's learning. The crisis creates a vicious cycle where the very tools that enable social mobility—good health and a solid education—are compromised, trapping the poor in poverty and further widening the already vast gap between the rich and the rest.

The Lost Middle Class and the Scars on the Psyche

One of the defining features of Argentina's social fabric was its large and aspirational middle class. For much of the 20th century, it was the bedrock of the nation's identity. The recurring crises have systematically hollowed out this group. Each wave of inflation and devaluation acts like a great wealth transfer, wiping out peso-denominated savings and pushing people down the economic ladder.

The psychological toll of this downward mobility is immense. It's the story of the small business owner who has to close the shop their family ran for generations. It's the professional who suddenly finds their university degree is not enough to keep them out of poverty. It's the constant anxiety of living in a world of profound economic uncertainty, where the value of your work and savings can be halved in an instant. This creates a society living on edge, marked by stress, distrust, and a deep-seated pessimism about the future. It fuels social and political polarization, as people search for someone to blame for their predicament.

The social contract frays. When the state is perceived as being unable to provide basic security or opportunity, people lose faith in institutions. This erosion of trust is one of the deepest and most difficult scars to heal. It makes the political consensus required for long-term, sustainable reforms almost impossible to achieve. The human cost, therefore, is not just measured in poverty rates, but in the loss of social cohesion and the dimming of collective hope. Argentina's recurring crises have left a legacy of not only economic debt, but a profound social and psychological deficit that continues to compound with each turn of the vicious cycle.

13.4 The Milei Experiment (2025): Shock Therapy and the Path to Stabilization

By the close of 2023, Argentina was a nation on the brink of complete economic combustion. Hyperinflation was no longer a threat; it was a daily reality. The peso had become a tragic joke, a currency whose value evaporated between morning coffee and the evening news. The state was a bloated, insolvent behemoth, kept alive only by the humming of the central bank's money-printing presses. Decades of populist promises, fiscal indiscipline, and failed stabilization plans had led the country to this precipice. The situation was not just critical; it felt terminal. It was in this atmosphere of desperation and national exhaustion that the Argentine people made a truly radical choice. They elected Javier Milei, a wild-haired libertarian economist who promised not just to reform the system, but to take a chainsaw to its very foundations.

What has unfolded since is one of the most audacious and closely-watched economic experiments in modern history. This is not a gentle, gradual adjustment. This is "shock therapy" in its purest and most brutal form. Milei's diagnosis of Argentina's illness was simple and uncompromising: the country was a chronic addict, hooked on the narcotic of state spending and the easy fix of printing money. The cure, he argued, could not be a gradual weaning off; it had to be a sudden, painful, cold-turkey detox. His program is built on two core, unwavering pillars. The first is the "motosierra," the chainsaw, a relentless and unapologetic assault on the fiscal deficit with the goal of achieving a surplus at all costs. The second is a wholesale deregulation of the economy, an attempt to untangle the suffocating knot of controls that had choked private enterprise for decades. It is a high-risk, high-reward strategy that, by 2025, has produced results as dramatic as the plan itself.

The Surgery: Wielding the Chainsaw

The first order of business for the new administration was to stop the bleeding. The primary cause of Argentina's hyperinflation was the simple fact that the government spent far, far more than it collected in revenue, and covered this massive shortfall by ordering the central bank to print new pesos. This firehose of freshly printed money chasing a limited supply of goods is the classic recipe for inflation. Milei's first move was to turn off the hose.

The chainsaw arrived. It was loud, brutal, and uncompromising. The number of government ministries was slashed in half overnight, a symbolic and substantive first cut. A freeze was put on all new public works projects, leaving half-finished roads and buildings as stark monuments to the new era of austerity. But the deepest and most painful cuts came to the vast web of subsidies that had kept the cost of daily life artificially low for millions. The prices of electricity, natural gas, and public transportation, long cushioned by the state, were allowed to surge towards their real market values. For the average citizen, this meant utility bills and bus fares that doubled, tripled, or even quadrupled in a matter of weeks.

This was the painful, front-loaded cost of the adjustment. But it was in service of a single, obsessive goal: achieving a fiscal surplus. For the first time in over a decade, the Argentine state was forced to live within its means. By the first quarter of 2025, the impossible had happened. The government announced a quarterly fiscal surplus, a small but seismic event. The state was taking in more money than it was spending. The money-printing presses had fallen silent. The primary engine of hyperinflation had been shut down.

Unleashing the Economy: Cutting the Red Tape

Running parallel to the fiscal surgery was an equally ambitious effort to deregulate the economy. Milei's team viewed Argentina as a caged animal, a powerhouse of potential trapped by decades of Peronist-inspired controls, protectionism, and bureaucracy. Their goal was to shatter the cage.

Through a series of emergency decrees and legislative packages, hundreds of regulations were wiped from the books. The notoriously complex and corrupt import licensing system was eliminated. The effect was immediate and visible. For years, buying an imported television or washing machine was a costly and difficult affair due to tariffs and restrictions. By 2025, with imports liberalized, shipping containers began to flow freely into the port of Buenos Aires. The price of home appliances was reported to have dropped by as much as 35%, a tangible benefit of the new policy for consumers.

The rental market, long governed by a law that imposed price caps and strict conditions, was completely deregulated. This gave landlords the freedom to set prices and contract terms, a move that, while controversial, was aimed at encouraging more properties to be offered for rent and ending the chronic shortages that plagued cities. From labor laws to land ownership, no corner of the regulated economy was safe from review. The philosophy was clear: get the state out of the way and let the market work.

The Verdict of 2025: A Shocking Success, A Fragile Peace

The initial results of this shock therapy have been nothing short of remarkable. The headline achievement is the taming of inflation. After spiking in the immediate aftermath of the initial devaluation, the monthly inflation rate began a steep and steady decline. By mid-2025, it had fallen to its lowest level in eight years, a stunning victory in the war against hyperinflation. For a society traumatized by constantly changing prices, the return of a semblance of price stability was a profound psychological relief.

The fiscal discipline held, and the markets took notice. The new IMF program was less a bailout and more a vote of confidence in a government that was over-delivering on its promises of austerity. The economy, after a severe initial contraction caused by the shock, began to show green shoots. The official projection for economic growth in 2025 was a robust 5.5%, a powerful rebound that supporters hailed as proof that the bitter medicine was working.

But this success rests on a knife's edge. The long-term challenges are monumental. The first and most pressing is the social cost. The chainsaw is not a precision instrument; it cuts deeply and painfully. With poverty rates having soared during the initial adjustment, the government faces the immense challenge of maintaining public support for a program that has imposed so much hardship. Social unrest and political backlash are a constant threat, a ticking clock that could force a reversal of the policies before they have time to bear long-term fruit.

Second is the complex monetary endgame. Taming inflation is one thing; building a stable and credible new monetary regime is another. The country still has a labyrinth of currency controls, and the government must navigate a path toward a unified, stable exchange rate without reigniting the inflationary fire it worked so hard to extinguish. Finally, there is the ultimate test: rebuilding credibility. One year of fiscal surpluses cannot erase a century of defaults and broken promises. To truly break the cycle, Argentina must regain the trust of international investors and, most importantly, of its own people. The Milei experiment has, against all odds, pulled Argentina back from the abyss. The question that hangs over the nation, and the world watching it, is whether this brutal, shocking, and so far successful surgery will lead to a lasting cure, or if it is merely a temporary remission in the country's long and recurring battle with its economic demons.

When Institutions Falter: The Perils of Politicized Monetary Policy in Turkey

14.1 The Erosion of Central Bank Independence

On paper, the Central Bank of the Republic of Turkey (CBRT) was a fortress. Forged in the fires of a devastating financial crisis in the early 2000s, its independence was enshrined in law in 2001. This was not merely a symbolic gesture; it was a core pillar of an ambitious, IMF-supported stabilization program designed to pull Turkey back from the brink. The new law granted the CBRT de jure, or legal, independence. It was given a clear and primary mandate: to achieve and maintain price stability. Its leadership was meant to be insulated from the whims of daily politics, empowered to make the tough, sometimes unpopular, decisions necessary to keep inflation in check. For a time, this framework worked, anchoring expectations and helping to usher in a period of remarkable economic growth and stability.

But a fortress, no matter how well-designed, is only as strong as the political will to respect its walls. The foundation of the CBRT's recent crisis lies in the systematic dismantling of this very respect. The story is a powerful lesson in the vast and often treacherous gap between the law as it is written and power as it is wielded. The legal shield of independence proved to be fragile, ultimately unable to withstand a sustained assault from a political leadership with a profoundly different economic ideology.

The erosion began in earnest after 2018, when Turkey transitioned to a new executive presidency system. This change concentrated immense power in the hands of President Recep Tayyip Erdoğan, who held a deeply entrenched and highly unorthodox economic belief.

Contrary to the consensus of mainstream economics practiced globally, the President championed the view that high interest rates were not the cure for inflation but its very cause. This "interest rate lobby," as he often termed it, was, in his view, strangling growth and burdening the nation. His goal was to foster a high-growth economy fueled by cheap credit, and the central bank's orthodox policy of raising rates to cool an overheating economy was a direct obstacle.

What followed was not a subtle campaign of influence but a direct and public assertion of political dominance over the monetary authority. President Erdoğan used his newly consolidated powers to appoint and, more critically, to dismiss the central bank's governor and senior leadership at will. This created a chilling effect, turning the governor's seat into a revolving door for anyone who dared to defy the President's vision.

The sequence of dismissals tells the story vividly. Governor Murat Çetinkaya was fired in mid-2019 for not cutting interest rates aggressively enough. His successor, Murat Uysal, obliged with a series of deep rate cuts but was himself dismissed in late 2020 as the Turkish Lira plummeted. The appointment of Naci Ağbal, a respected former finance minister, seemed to signal a brief return to orthodoxy. Ağbal immediately and aggressively raised interest rates, attempting to restore the bank's shattered credibility and tame runaway inflation. The markets cheered. Yet, just four months into his tenure, after a decisive rate hike, he too was summarily fired in a shocking overnight decree.

His removal was the point of no return. It was the clearest possible signal to both domestic and international observers: the CBRT was no longer an independent institution. Its technical judgments, its legal mandate, and its economic analyses were secondary to the political directives emanating from the presidential palace. The concept of de facto independence—the actual, lived reality of the bank's autonomy—was utterly destroyed. The laws granting independence remained on the books, but they had been hollowed out, leaving an empty shell. Credibility, the most precious asset of any central bank, evaporated. This loss of trust was the essential precondition for the full-blown crisis that would follow, as it meant the bank was now powerless to anchor the public's expectations about future inflation, setting the stage for a catastrophic economic experiment.

14.2 The "Turkish Experiment": Unorthodox Monetary Policy in Action

With the guardrails of central bank independence torn away, the path was cleared for one of the most audacious and dangerous economic gambles of the 21st century. This wasn't a subtle shift in policy or a minor course correction. It was a full-scale, real-world experiment based on a radical economic theory, with the livelihoods of over 85 million people hanging in the balance. The world watched, with a mixture of curiosity and alarm, as Turkey deliberately steered its ship of state directly into a hurricane, convinced it had discovered a new way to sail.

The starting pistol for this "Turkish experiment" fired in the autumn of 2021. At the time, inflation was already uncomfortably high, creeping toward 20%. Across the globe, from the U.S. Federal Reserve to the European Central Bank, policymakers were sounding the alarm about rising prices and laying the groundwork to raise interest rates—the standard, time-tested medicine for cooling an overheating economy. Turkey's leadership, however, chose this exact moment to sprint in the opposite direction. Under immense pressure from the presidential palace, the new leadership at the CBRT began to slash interest rates. In a dizzying series of moves over just a few months, the main policy rate was chopped from 19% all the way down to 14%.

To an economist, this was like pouring gasoline on a raging fire. But in the minds of its architects, the logic was simple, seductive, and profoundly heterodox. The core belief, championed relentlessly by President Erdoğan, was that the conventional wisdom had it all backward. High interest rates, the theory went, were not the cure for inflation; they were the cause. The argument was that high rates increased the cost of borrowing for businesses. These businesses, burdened by higher financing costs, would then pass those costs onto consumers in the form of higher prices. Therefore, to break the inflationary cycle, one had to first cut the costs for producers. Lowering interest rates would make credit cheap, encouraging companies to borrow, invest, expand production, and hire more workers. This surge in supply, combined with lower business costs, would ultimately lead to lower prices and booming exports, creating a current account surplus and a stronger, more resilient economy. It was a vision of painless growth, a shortcut to prosperity that defied the textbooks.

The world didn't have to wait long to see the results of this grand hypothesis. The "Turkish experiment" served as a brutal, unintentional, and large-scale empirical test, and the verdict was swift and damning: it was a catastrophic failure. Instead of a virtuous cycle of growth, the policy unleashed a vicious spiral of economic chaos, precisely as mainstream macroeconomic models would have predicted.

The first and most immediate consequence was the collapse of the Turkish Lira. For savers and investors, both in Turkey and abroad, the decision was simple arithmetic.

With inflation running near 20% and interest rates cut to 14%, holding money in a Lira account meant guaranteeing a significant loss in real terms. The real interest rate was deeply negative. People scrambled to protect their wealth. There was a massive, panicked flight from the Lira as individuals and companies dumped the currency and bought safer assets, primarily U.S. dollars and euros. This exodus caused the Lira's value to plummet on international markets.

This currency depreciation then acted as a powerful accelerant for inflation. The Turkish economy is deeply intertwined with the rest of the world, relying heavily on imported goods—most critically, energy like oil and natural gas, but also raw materials and components for its vast manufacturing sector. As the Lira crashed, the cost of every single imported item soared. A tanker of oil that cost a certain amount in dollars now required vastly more Lira to purchase. This surge in import costs fed directly and immediately into domestic prices. Gas prices at the pump shot up, electricity bills climbed, and the cost of producing almost everything, from textiles to cars, increased, pushing consumer prices ever higher.

This is where the psychological damage began. The process completely un-anchored inflation expectations. Seeing prices rise daily and the value of their savings evaporate, people lost all faith that the authorities had the will or the ability to restore stability. The expectation that prices would continue to spiral upwards became a self-fulfilling prophecy. Businesses started raising their prices proactively, trying to get ahead of their own rising costs. Workers demanded massive wage hikes just to keep their heads above water. A "buy now" mentality took hold, as everyone tried to spend their money before it lost even more of its value. This created a full-blown hyperinflationary spiral. The very policy designed to lower inflation had ignited it, sending it rocketing to a peak of over 85% by the end of 2022.

The scale of the policy-induced damage is not just a matter of observation; it can be quantified. Economists using a sophisticated statistical technique called the synthetic control method have tried to answer the question: what would have happened if Turkey had stuck to orthodox policy? This method creates a "counterfactual" or "synthetic" Turkey by building a weighted average of similar emerging-market countries that acted conventionally during this period—countries that raised interest rates to fight inflation. The results of this analysis are stark. They suggest that while Turkey would have still faced inflationary pressures from global events, its inflation rate would likely have remained in the neighborhood of 20%. The vast chasm between that 20% figure and the devastating 85% peak represents the direct, measurable, and painful cost of the "Turkish experiment." It was a self-inflicted wound of historic proportions.

14.3 The Economic Consequences: Hyperinflation, Currency Collapse, and Financial Instability

If the unorthodox experiment was the theoretical blueprint, its real-world construction was an economic earthquake. The consequences were not abstract, academic, or delayed. They were immediate, brutal, and felt in the daily lives of every single person in the country. The tremors of the policy shift quickly became a full-blown seismic event, shaking the very foundations of Turkish society and leaving a landscape of financial ruin and deep-seated uncertainty.

The first and most visible casualty was the Turkish Lira. It did not decline; it capitulated. The currency went into an uncontrolled freefall, a spectacle of collapsing confidence broadcast in real-time on foreign exchange markets. For ordinary citizens, this was not just a number on a screen. It was a daily erosion of their past, present, and future. A salary that was adequate one month could barely cover necessities the next. The savings meticulously accumulated over a lifetime, intended for a child's education or a comfortable retirement, were decimated in a matter of months, their purchasing power melting away like ice on a summer pavement. The Lira lost more than half its value against the U.S. dollar in the initial, chaotic months. But the slide didn't stop. It became a relentless, grinding depreciation that continued for years, a constant reminder of the instability that now defined the economy. By late 2025, the currency had breached the once-unthinkable level of 41 to the dollar, a stark numerical tombstone for a generation's worth of value.

This currency collapse was the kindling for a raging inflationary inferno. As the Lira's value evaporated, the cost of everything imported—and in a globalized economy, that means almost everything—skyrocketed. The price of fuel, a lifeblood for transportation and industry, surged. The cost of raw materials for factories, wheat for bread, and medicine for the sick all followed suit. This tsunami of imported costs crashed into the domestic economy, and businesses, struggling to survive, had no choice but to pass them on to consumers.

The result was a hyperinflationary spiral that tore through the social fabric. In October 2022, official consumer price inflation peaked at a staggering 85.5%, a level unseen in over two decades. This number fails to capture the sheer chaos of the experience. It meant that prices were no longer stable reference points but moving targets. A trip to the grocery store became an exercise in shock and anxiety, with prices for basics like cheese, cooking oil, and milk visibly higher than the week before. Restaurants stopped printing menus, opting for chalkboards or QR codes that could be updated daily. The fundamental trust that money holds its value from one day to the next was shattered. This environment punished savers and rewarded debtors, turning sensible financial planning on its head and forcing millions to live in a state of perpetual economic insecurity. Even as the initial peak of the crisis passed, the damage was done. Inflation became a chronic disease, a stubborn poison in the economic bloodstream that proved incredibly difficult to remove, still standing at an painfully high 33.29% as late as September 2025.

Faced with a full-blown panic and a run on the Lira, but ideologically unwilling to use the only effective tool—raising interest rates—the government scrambled for an alternative. In late 2021, they unveiled a desperate and novel financial instrument, a scheme that would have monumental consequences: the "currency-protected deposit scheme," known colloquially as KKM. The offer to the public was deceptively simple: keep your money in a Turkish Lira deposit account, and the government will guarantee it. If the Lira depreciates against the U.S. dollar by more than the interest you earn, the Treasury and Central Bank will pay you the difference.

On the surface, it seemed like a clever workaround. It offered citizens a way to hold Lira without fear of currency risk, and for a short time, it did manage to slow the frantic stampede into dollars. But in reality, the KKM scheme was an act of profound fiscal recklessness. It did not eliminate the currency risk; it simply transferred it. The immense, volatile risk of the foreign exchange market was lifted from the shoulders of private individuals and placed squarely onto the public balance sheet—onto the backs of all taxpayers.

The government was essentially making a massive, unhedged bet against its own currency. If the Lira continued to fall, the public purse would be on the hook for colossal payouts. And fall it did. The bill for this gamble soon came due, and it was astronomical. The Central Bank, which was forced to backstop the program, saw its finances obliterated. In 2023, the CBRT recorded a net loss of over 818 billion Lira, an almost incomprehensible sum, with the vast majority of it directly attributable to payments made to prop up the KKM scheme. This wasn't just a monetary policy failure; it had morphed into a fiscal crisis. It blurred the lines between the central bank and the treasury, forcing the institution mandated to fight inflation to print money to cover the losses from a scheme designed to avoid fighting inflation. This unorthodox solution created a hidden and utterly unsustainable national debt, jeopardizing the long-term solvency of the state itself.

The cumulative effect of the currency collapse, the hyperinflation, and the fiscally ruinous KKM scheme was the utter destruction of investor confidence. The predictable, stable, rules-based economic environment that investors crave had been replaced by a system governed by impulse and ideological dogma. Foreign capital, once a key driver of Turkish growth, fled the country in droves. International investors sold their stocks and bonds and repatriated their money, unwilling to gamble in such a volatile market. Domestic businesses, seeing the chaos, also moved their capital abroad, seeking a safe haven from the storm at home. The "Turkish experiment" had not only failed to produce the promised boom; it had repelled the very capital and confidence needed for any sustainable growth, leaving the economy isolated, unstable, and facing a long, arduous road to recovery.

14.4 The Painful Return to Orthodoxy

After years of driving against all the warning signs, the economic engine of Turkey finally seized. The damage was too extensive, the public's pain too acute, and the international isolation too complete to ignore any longer. The unorthodox experiment, born of a deep-seated conviction, had crashed against the unyielding wall of economic reality. The aftermath of President Erdoğan's re-election in mid-2023 marked the beginning of a humbling and arduous journey back—a reluctant, politically fraught, and painful return to the very economic principles that had been so publicly scorned.

The first signal of this monumental U-turn was the appointment of a new, internationally respected economic team. This was more than a personnel change; it was a white flag. It was a tacit admission that the previous path had led to a dead end. The new leadership at the Central Bank and the Treasury was tasked with an almost impossible mission: to clean up the wreckage, restore a semblance of order, and somehow regain the trust of a deeply skeptical world and a weary domestic population.

Their first actions had to be decisive. There was no room for half-measures. To signal that the era of make-believe economics was truly over, the CBRT immediately fell upon the primary tool of orthodox monetary policy: the interest rate. With inflation still raging and the currency still fragile, they initiated one of the most aggressive and dramatic monetary tightening cycles in modern economic history. In a series of bold, powerful steps, the policy rate was hoisted from its artificially low level of 8.5% all the way up to a staggering 46%.

Each rate hike was a shockwave sent through the economy, a dose of harsh but necessary medicine. The goal was twofold. First, and most urgently, it was to break the back of the hyperinflationary spiral. By making it extremely expensive to borrow money, the high rates were designed to cool down superheated demand, forcing businesses and consumers to pull back on spending. This would, in theory, put the brakes on soaring prices. Second, the hikes were a desperate act of communication—a costly signal to international markets that Turkey was, at long last, serious about restoring credibility. It was a message that the central bank was once again independent, empowered to make painful decisions, and committed to its primary mandate of achieving price stability.

But this medicine, while essential, is also a potent poison for economic growth. The return to orthodoxy is not a triumphant march but a painful slog through a recessionary valley. The same sky-high interest rates needed to kill inflation also kill economic dynamism. For years, the Turkish economy had been addicted to cheap credit, a powerful stimulant that fueled construction booms and consumer spending. Suddenly, that tap was turned off. Businesses that had planned to expand or invest were now faced with crippling borrowing costs, forcing them to shelve their plans. Small and medium-sized enterprises struggled to access the credit they needed just to manage their daily operations. Mortgages and car loans became prohibitively expensive, causing consumer spending to grind to a halt.

This created an excruciating political trade-off for a government that had built its entire identity and popular support on delivering high rates of economic growth. For over a decade, the political narrative had been simple: growth above all else. Now, the government's own economic team was deliberately engineering a slowdown. The political pressure was, and remains, immense. Every factory that lays off workers, every shop that closes its doors, and every family that defaults on a loan adds to the public's discontent. The very architects of the unorthodox experiment are now forced to administer the painful cure, testing the limits of their political resilience.

The inherent fragility of this new path was starkly illustrated in 2025. Just as a fragile sense of stability was beginning to take root, a political storm erupted. The arrest of a prominent opposition figure on contentious charges sent a tremor of political risk through the financial markets. The reaction was instantaneous and reflexive. Investors, their confidence still paper-thin, began to pull their money out. This capital outflow put immediate, renewed pressure on the Turkish Lira, threatening to undo months of hard-won stabilization.

This episode served as a brutal lesson in the asymmetry of credibility. Credibility is like a grand old tree that takes a century to grow but can be chopped down in a single afternoon. Turkey's leaders had spent years hacking away at the credibility of their economic institutions. Rebuilding it is a far slower and more delicate process. It requires not just a few correct policy moves but a long, uninterrupted period of consistent, predictable, and unwavering conduct. Every single action—every speech, every data release, every political appointment—is now placed under a microscope by global markets, which remain deeply scarred and perpetually on edge. A single perceived misstep, a hint of a return to old habits, or a sign of political interference could shatter the fragile new confidence in an instant.

Ultimately, the Turkish saga stands as one of the clearest and most powerful cautionary tales in recent economic history. It is a real-world, high-stakes demonstration of a timeless truth: that credible, independent institutions are not a luxury but the absolute bedrock of long-term macroeconomic stability and prosperity. They are the essential guardrails that protect an economy from the powerful and often short-sighted temptations of politics. Turkey is now on the long road back, a journey that will require immense patience from its people and unwavering resolve from its policymakers. The world watches, not with scorn, but with the hope that the lessons of this painful chapter have been truly and permanently learned.

The Resource Curse and the Challenge of Economic Diversification: The Nigerian Case

Nigeria, Africa's most populous nation and one of its largest economies, provides a classic and sobering case study of the "resource curse." The discovery of vast oil reserves transformed the country's economy but also exposed it to extreme volatility, fueled corruption, and hindered broader development. This chapter examines the history of Nigeria's oil dependence and the onset of "Dutch Disease," the complex interaction of monetary and fiscal policy in a resource-rich economy, the profound social and political consequences of the resource curse, and the persistent challenges of achieving meaningful economic diversification.

15.1 The History of Oil Discovery and the Onset of "Dutch Disease"

The story of modern Nigeria's economy is inextricably linked to a single discovery. In 1956, in a small community called Oloibiri in the Niger Delta, oil was found in commercially viable quantities. This moment marked a fundamental turning point, setting the nation on a new and perilous economic path. Before this, Nigeria's economy was grounded in the earth. Agriculture was its backbone, providing the primary source of government income, jobs, and foreign exchange. The country was a major exporter of cocoa, palm oil, and groundnuts.

But the lure of "black gold" was powerful. As oil production ramped up through the 1960s and especially during the oil boom of the 1970s, everything changed. The revenue flowing into the government's coffers from oil exports was staggering, dwarfing anything agriculture could produce. Quickly, the nation's focus shifted. Agriculture was neglected, and the country's economic fortunes became tied to the volatile price of a single commodity on the global market.

This sudden influx of wealth triggered a classic economic phenomenon known as "Dutch Disease." The term was coined to describe a similar situation in the Netherlands after a large natural gas discovery. In Nigeria's case, the massive amounts of foreign currency from oil sales caused the value of the local currency, the Naira, to strengthen significantly.

On the surface, a strong currency might sound like a good thing. But for Nigeria, it was a disaster for every other sector of the economy. The strong Naira made Nigerian agricultural and manufactured goods much more expensive for other countries to buy. As a result, its traditional exports became uncompetitive on the world stage. At the same time, it became much cheaper to import goods from other countries.

The consequences were devastating and swift. The once-thriving agricultural sector collapsed. Its share of total exports plummeted from over 40% in 1970 to less than 3% just fifteen years later. Local manufacturing industries found they couldn't compete with the flood of cheaper imported products. This led to a process of de-industrialization, where local factories and businesses shut down. Nigeria stopped being a country that made things and grew things, and instead became a nation that simply extracted one resource and used the money to buy everything else it needed. It had become a classic mono-economy, dangerously dependent on oil and completely vulnerable to the unpredictable swings in its price.

15.2 The Dance of Monetary and Fiscal Policy

In a country overwhelmed by oil revenue, managing the nation's finances becomes a monumental challenge. For Nigeria, both monetary and fiscal policy have been profoundly shaped—and often distorted—by the boom-and-bust cycles of the global oil market. The country's approach to spending its oil wealth has been largely procyclical, which is a technical way of saying the government spends lavishly when oil prices are high and then is forced into painful austerity when they crash.

This creates a rollercoaster of economic instability. During oil booms, government spending explodes. Money is poured into ambitious infrastructure projects, the civil service expands, and subsidies are introduced. This sudden injection of cash often leads to high inflation, making the cost of living soar for ordinary citizens. However, because this spending is not based on a stable, diversified economy, it is unsustainable.

When the inevitable oil price crash occurs, the government's revenue dries up. Projects are abandoned, public sector salaries go unpaid, and the government finds itself in a deep fiscal crisis. This boom-bust cycle makes long-term economic planning almost impossible. It's difficult for businesses to invest and grow when the economic environment is so unpredictable.

A major part of the problem has been the absence of effective fiscal rules to manage the volatility. While some mechanisms, like the Excess Crude Account, were created to save money during boom times, they have often been undermined by political pressure to spend. The revenue-sharing formula, which distributes oil income among the federal, state, and local governments, further complicates matters. It creates an expectation that the money will be shared and spent immediately, rather than saved for a rainy day or invested in long-term development.

Furthermore, the management of oil revenues has been plagued by a lack of transparency and widespread corruption. The Nigerian National Petroleum Corporation (NNPC), the state-owned oil company, has long been criticized for its opaque operations. Billions of dollars in oil revenue have been mismanaged or have simply gone missing over the decades, depriving the nation of funds that could have been used for education, healthcare, and critical infrastructure. This fiscal indiscipline, combined with a monetary policy often forced to react to the government's spending habits, has trapped Nigeria in a cycle of instability that directly hinders its path toward a more diversified and resilient economy.

15.3 The Profound Social and Political Consequences

The resource curse is more than just an economic phenomenon; it has deeply wounded Nigeria's social and political fabric. The vast, unearned wealth flowing from oil fundamentally changed the relationship between the government and its people. In most countries, governments rely on taxes from their citizens to function. This creates a bond of accountability; people pay taxes and, in return, demand services and responsible governance.

In Nigeria, oil revenue broke this bond. The government became less dependent on its people and more dependent on oil companies. This created a "rentier state," where the government's main activity became the distribution of oil rents rather than the cultivation of a productive economy. As a result, accountability vanished. Politicians and officials felt they were not answerable to the citizens, leading to a culture of impunity and staggering levels of corruption. Politics became a zero-sum game, where the primary goal was to gain control of the state and its access to oil wealth.

This has had devastating social consequences. The immense oil wealth has never been shared equitably. While a small elite became fantastically rich, the majority of Nigerians have remained trapped in poverty. This created a paradox of poverty in the midst of plenty, fueling deep-seated public anger and resentment.

Nowhere has this been felt more acutely than in the Niger Delta, the very region from which the oil is extracted. For decades, local communities have seen their land and rivers polluted by oil spills and gas flaring, destroying their traditional livelihoods of farming and fishing. Yet, they have received very few of the benefits. The region suffers from a lack of basic infrastructure like clean water, electricity, schools, and hospitals.

This profound sense of injustice and neglect led to the rise of militancy. Frustrated and disenfranchised, various groups have taken up arms, demanding a greater share of the oil wealth and compensation for the environmental damage. Their tactics have included kidnapping oil workers, sabotaging pipelines, and fighting government forces. This conflict has not only caused immense human suffering but has also disrupted oil production, further destabilizing the national economy. The resource curse, therefore, has not just hindered economic growth; it has actively fueled division, conflict, and social decay.

15.4 The Persistent Challenges of Economic Diversification

For decades, every Nigerian government has spoken about the need for economic diversification. They all recognize the danger of relying on a single commodity. Yet, achieving this goal has proven to be an incredibly persistent and difficult challenge. The very structure of the oil-dependent economy creates powerful forces that resist change.

One of the biggest hurdles is the severe lack of infrastructure. To build a thriving manufacturing or agricultural sector, you need reliable electricity, good roads, and efficient ports. Nigeria is chronically deficient in all of these areas. The power supply is notoriously unreliable, forcing businesses to spend huge sums on private generators, which dramatically increases their operating costs and makes them uncompetitive. Moving goods around the country is slow and expensive due to a dilapidated road network.

A second major challenge lies in the political and institutional environment. The political system, long accustomed to distributing oil rents, lacks the discipline and long-term vision required for the hard work of economic transformation. Policymaking is often inconsistent and focused on short-term crisis management rather than on implementing the deep, structural reforms needed. Corruption remains a massive obstacle, diverting funds that are meant for development and creating an uneven playing field where connections matter more than innovation and efficiency.

Furthermore, the years of neglect have taken a toll on other sectors. The agricultural sector is dominated by small-scale farmers using outdated methods, with limited access to modern technology, credit, or training. The manufacturing sector struggles not only with infrastructure deficits but also with a difficult regulatory environment and a workforce that often lacks the necessary skills.

Ultimately, the political will to enact real change is often undermined by the very oil wealth it seeks to move away from. It has always been easier for those in power to focus on controlling and distributing oil revenue than to undertake the complex, long-term project of building a truly productive and diversified economy. Breaking this cycle requires more than just economic policies; it requires a fundamental shift in political culture and a sustained commitment to building the strong, transparent institutions that can support a vibrant, post-oil future for Nigeria.

15.2 The Unsteady Dance: Monetary and Fiscal Policy in Nigeria's Oil-Fueled Economy

Imagine trying to steer a ship through a hurricane, where the storm's intensity changes without warning. One moment, fierce winds and towering waves threaten to capsize you; the next, an eerie calm descends, leaving you stranded. This is the reality for the architects of Nigeria's economic policy. The "hurricane" is the global oil market, and the ship is the nation's economy. The two captains trying to navigate this storm are the fiscal authorities (the government, represented by the Ministry of Finance) and the monetary authorities (the Central Bank of Nigeria, or CBN). Their relationship, a complex and often strained dance, lies at the very heart of why Nigeria has struggled to convert its immense oil wealth into lasting prosperity for its people.

The fundamental problem is one of rhythm. In a healthy, diversified economy, fiscal and monetary policies often work in a counter-cyclical rhythm. When the economy slows down, the government might spend more (fiscal stimulus) and the central bank might lower interest rates (monetary stimulus) to encourage growth. When the economy overheats, they do the opposite to cool things down. Nigeria's oil dependency forces it into the exact opposite pattern: a procyclical one. The government's behavior is dictated not by the needs of its people or its domestic economy, but by the price of a barrel of Brent crude oil. This creates a devastating "boom-bust" cycle that holds the nation's development hostage.

The Boom: A Torrent of Cash and Perilous Choices

When global oil prices soar, a flood of US dollars pours into Nigeria's government accounts. On the surface, this feels like winning the lottery. Revenue swells, and a sense of boundless optimism takes hold. This is the "boom" phase, and it is a period of great peril disguised as prosperity.

The government's immediate response is almost always the same: spend, and spend big. This spending spree is the fiscal side of the dance. The federal budget expands dramatically. Ambitious, often poorly planned, infrastructure projects are announced with great fanfare. The public sector wage bill balloons as more people are hired into government jobs. Subsidies, especially for fuel, are introduced or increased, presented as a way to share the wealth with the populace.

This sudden, massive injection of cash creates enormous problems. It's like trying to force the entire flow of a river through a garden hose. The economy simply cannot absorb the money productively. The result is often high inflation. With more money chasing the same amount of goods and services, prices for everything from food to rent begin to skyrocket, hurting ordinary citizens the most. The very wealth that was meant to help them ends up eroding their purchasing power.

This is where the Central Bank of Nigeria (CBN) steps in, attempting the monetary side of the dance. The CBN sees the inflationary storm gathering and knows it must act. Its primary challenge is managing the deluge of foreign currency. All those oil dollars need to be converted into

Naira for the government to spend, which massively increases the money supply and puts intense upward pressure on the value of the local currency. This strengthening Naira is the core symptom of "Dutch Disease," making Nigeria's other exports uncompetitive and imports artificially cheap.

The CBN is forced to perform a difficult balancing act. It tries to "sterilize" the inflows, essentially selling government bonds to mop up the excess Naira from the banking system to curb inflation. But this is a monumental task. The sheer volume of oil revenue can overwhelm its capacity. Furthermore, it finds itself dancing to a completely different tune than the government. While the Ministry of Finance is flooring the spending accelerator, the CBN is trying to slam on the monetary brakes. This fundamental conflict between expansionary fiscal policy and contractionary monetary policy creates immense instability and sends confusing signals to the entire economy.

The Bust: The Inevitable Crash and Painful Austerity

The global oil market is notoriously fickle. The boom never lasts. When prices inevitably crash, Nigeria's economic reality shifts from a flood to a devastating drought. The government's revenue stream, once a torrent, slows to a trickle. This is the "bust," and the consequences are brutal.

The fiscal authorities, having built a structure of expenditure based on high oil prices, find themselves in a state of panic. The music has stopped, but the bills are still due. The ambitious infrastructure projects grind to a halt, leaving behind a landscape of unfinished roads, bridges, and buildings—monuments to unsustainable planning. Public sector salaries, which were easy to pay during the boom, suddenly become an unbearable burden, often going unpaid for months. The generous subsidies become impossible to afford, and the government is forced into a period of sharp, painful austerity.

This fiscal contraction sends shockwaves through the economy, often tipping it into recession. Government is the largest spender in the Nigerian economy, and when it stops spending, everyone feels the pain. Businesses that relied on government contracts collapse. Jobs are lost. Public services deteriorate.

The CBN, once again, is caught in the crisis. Its focus shifts dramatically. During the boom, it was worried about a currency that was too strong; during the bust, it desperately tries to prevent a currency collapse. Foreign exchange reserves, which seemed plentiful during the good times, are rapidly depleted as the country continues to pay for imports while its main source of dollars has dried up.

Here, a dangerous phenomenon known as "fiscal dominance" often takes hold. The government, starved for cash and unable to borrow easily from international markets, turns to its last resort: the central bank. It pressures the CBN to finance its budget deficits. This is often a polite term for printing money. This act severely compromises the central bank's independence and its core mission to control inflation. When a central bank is forced to finance government spending, it loses control over the money supply, which can lead to runaway inflation and a complete loss of confidence in the currency and the economy.

A Dysfunctional Partnership: The Institutional Failings

The perpetual boom-bust cycle is not just an accident of the market; it is cemented by deep institutional weaknesses. The coordination between the fiscal and monetary authorities is consistently poor. They are supposed to be partners in managing the economy, but their conflicting pressures often make them adversaries.

A prime example of this failure is the management of savings. Logically, a country dependent on a volatile commodity should be obsessive about saving money during the good times to cushion the bad times. Nigeria has tried to create mechanisms for this, most notably the Excess Crude Account (ECA), designed to save oil revenue earned above a benchmark price. In theory, the ECA is a perfect tool for a counter-cyclical fiscal policy.

In practice, it has been largely ineffective. The immense political pressure to spend is overwhelming. The revenue-sharing formula that distributes income among the federal, state, and local governments creates a powerful incentive to share and spend the money immediately. State governors often argue that the savings are constitutionally theirs to spend now, not to be held by the federal government for a future crisis. This, combined with a severe lack of transparency and allegations of mismanagement, has meant that the account is frequently depleted just when it is needed most. The national savings jar is almost always empty when the rain stops falling.

This failure to save leaves the country brutally exposed to every price shock and ensures that the cycle of frantic spending followed by painful austerity continues indefinitely. It makes long-term economic planning a near-impossible fantasy. How can a business owner invest in a new factory when they have no idea if the economy will be booming or in a deep recession next year? How can the nation build the schools and hospitals it needs when the funding for them can evaporate overnight? This volatility, driven by the dysfunctional dance of monetary and fiscal policy, is perhaps the single greatest obstacle to

Nigeria's quest for sustainable development and economic diversification. It is a self-inflicted wound, repeated over and over, that keeps the giant of Africa from reaching its true potential.

15.3 The Poisoned Chalice: Nigeria's Social and Political Fabric Under the Resource Curse

Imagine a family that discovers a treasure chest buried in their backyard. The chest is bottomless, constantly refilling with gold coins. At first, there is celebration. But soon, the family stops tending their garden, stops fixing their home, stops talking to one another. Their entire existence becomes consumed by one question: who gets the next handful of gold? The siblings become rivals, trust evaporates, and the house falls into disrepair while they fight over the treasure. This is the story of Nigeria. The discovery of oil was the discovery of a bottomless treasure chest, but it has proven to be a poisoned chalice. The economic damage, as devastating as it is, pales in comparison to the deep wounds inflicted upon the nation's very soul—its society and its politics.

The resource curse is more than just an economic theory; in Nigeria, it is a lived reality that has fundamentally warped the relationship between the government and its people, turned politics into a dangerous winner-take-all contest, and created a heartbreaking paradox of mass poverty in one of the world's most resource-rich nations.

The Great Disconnect: How Oil Broke the Bond Between the Rulers and the Ruled

In most functioning societies, there is an unspoken, essential contract between the government and its citizens. The people pay taxes, and in return, the government is obligated to provide services: schools for their children, hospitals for their sick, roads for their businesses, and security for their families. This dependency creates accountability. If a government fails to deliver, the people can protest, vote them out, and demand better, because their tax money is the lifeblood of the state.

In Nigeria, oil revenue shattered this sacred bond.

The Nigerian government, for decades, has not needed its people's taxes to survive. Its lifeblood comes not from the millions of farmers, traders, and workers across the country, but from a handful of multinational oil corporations drilling in the Niger Delta. This creates what political scientists call a "rentier state"—a state that lives off unearned "rents" from a natural resource rather than the productive capacity of its citizens.

The consequences of this are profound and devastating. The government's accountability shifts. Its primary stakeholders are no longer its 200 million citizens, but the oil companies. It becomes less a government of the people and more a manager of oil contracts. This creates a massive psychological and political disconnect. The leaders in Abuja feel little pressure to perform for the people, because their political survival and personal enrichment depend on controlling the flow of oil money, not on earning the public's trust or support.

This disconnect fosters a culture of breathtaking impunity. When citizens complain about the lack of electricity or the terrible state of the roads, their cries fall on deaf ears. The government has no incentive to fix these problems because fixing them doesn't affect its bottom line. The money will keep flowing from the oil wells regardless. This has transformed the Nigerian state from a provider of public goods into a distributor of private wealth for the connected elite, leaving the vast majority of its people to fend for themselves.

The "National Cake": How Corruption Became the Operating System

When the state's primary function is to distribute a massive pot of unearned money, politics ceases to be about public service. It becomes a ruthless, high-stakes battle to control the pot. In Nigeria, oil revenue is often referred to as the "national cake." The overriding goal of the political system has become getting the biggest possible slice of this cake.

This has fueled a level of corruption that is systemic and all-consuming. It is not just a few bad apples; it has become the very operating system of the state. "Rent-seeking" is the term for this—when people focus their efforts on manipulating the system to get a share of existing wealth rather than creating new wealth. In Nigeria, it is the national sport. Instead of building innovative businesses, pioneering new technologies, or improving agricultural yields, the quickest path to unimaginable wealth is through a government contract, an oil license, or a political appointment.

This has had a cancerous effect on governance and institutions. Ministries that should be focused on health or education become centers for contract fraud. The police force, underfunded and poorly managed, is often seen by its officers as an opportunity for personal enrichment through bribes. The judiciary, which should be the last bastion of justice, can be compromised, with judgments for sale to the highest bidder. Every institution is weakened because its purpose is subverted. The goal is no longer to serve the public, but to extract resources for private gain.

This makes politics a zero-sum game of extreme consequence. Elections are not just contests of ideas; they are wars for the control of the treasury. The stakes are so high that violence, intimidation, and rigging become commonplace. The winner doesn't just get to govern; they get control of the oil taps, which means access to billions of dollars. The loser gets nothing. This desperate struggle for power further destabilizes the country, making peaceful transfers of power and long-term policymaking incredibly difficult.

The Niger Delta: A Land Drowning in Oil and Blood

Nowhere are the social consequences of the resource curse more tragically visible than in the Niger Delta, the very source of Nigeria's wealth. For the communities living on the creeks and swamps from which the oil is pumped, the resource has not been a blessing, but a relentless curse that has stolen their livelihoods, poisoned their environment, and fueled decades of violent conflict.

For generations, the people of the Delta were fishermen and farmers. The oil boom destroyed this way of life. Constant oil spills have coated rivers and farmland with a black sheen, killing the fish and rendering the soil infertile. Gas flaring—the burning of excess natural gas—roars day and night, polluting the air and causing acid rain that corrodes the roofs of their homes. These communities see pipelines carrying billions of dollars of wealth crisscross their ancestral lands, while they themselves lack the most basic amenities: clean drinking water, electricity, functioning schools, or clinics.

This created a profound and explosive sense of injustice. A generation of young people grew up seeing their environment destroyed and their future stolen, with no share in the wealth being extracted from beneath their feet. This anger and desperation gave rise to militancy. Armed groups emerged, demanding a greater share of the oil revenue and compensation for the environmental devastation. Their tactics—kidnapping oil workers, sabotaging pipelines, and engaging in armed conflict with government forces—have cost countless lives and have periodically crippled Nigeria's oil production, sending shockwaves through the national economy.

The conflict has created a vicious cycle of violence and repression. The government's response has often been heavy-handed military crackdowns, which further alienate the local population and serve as a recruiting tool for the militant groups. The oil wealth, instead of developing the region, has militarized it, turning it into a place of fear, instability, and deep-seated grievance. The tragic irony is that the people living on top of one of the world's largest oil reserves remain among the poorest and most neglected in the country. Their suffering is the starkest evidence of the resource curse's human cost.

15.4 The Architect's Dilemma: Blueprint for a Nigeria Beyond Oil

For as long as anyone can remember, "economic diversification" has been the most repeated phrase in the halls of power in Nigeria. It is the promised land, the cure for the nation's chronic illness of oil dependency. Every new government, every finance minister, and every five-year plan has championed it as the ultimate goal. Plans with hopeful acronyms, like the Economic Recovery and Growth Plan (ERGP), have been launched with great fanfare. Yet, after decades of talk, Nigeria remains, in its economic soul, an oil nation. The journey from rhetoric to reality has been agonizingly slow, and the reasons why reveal a challenge that is as much about human behavior and political will as it is about economic theory.

Breaking the resource curse isn't about finding a single magic bullet. It's like renovating a house that is actively sinking into the ground. You cannot simply start painting the walls and adding new furniture. You must first fix the broken, unstable foundation, and only then can you begin the long, difficult work of building something new and durable on top of it. For Nigeria, this means tackling the problem on two simultaneous fronts: first, fundamentally changing how it manages its oil wealth, and second, creating a fertile ground where a new, vibrant, non-oil economy can finally grow.

Part 1: Fixing the Sinking Foundation - Reforming the Oil Economy

Before Nigeria can dream of a future in tech, manufacturing, or agribusiness, it must tame the monster in its own house: the corrupt and volatile system of managing oil revenue. As long as this system remains broken, any money allocated for diversification will simply be consumed by the same old problems.

The First Commandment: Transparency and Governance

The single greatest obstacle to progress is corruption. The management of Nigeria's oil revenue has for decades been shrouded in secrecy, making it a playground for corrupt officials. The Nigerian National Petroleum Corporation (NNPC), the state entity that manages the nation's oil interests, has long been a black box, its finances opaque and its operations unaccountable to the public. Billions of dollars have vanished through shady fuel subsidy schemes, rigged contracts, and the outright theft of crude oil.

Therefore, the first and most critical policy is radical transparency. This isn't just a moral imperative; it's an economic necessity. The government must throw open the books. This means implementing and enforcing initiatives like the Extractive Industries Transparency Initiative (EITI), which requires the publication of all payments made by oil companies to the government. It means a complete, independent, and public audit of the NNPC. When the public can see exactly how much money is coming in and where it is going, it becomes much harder for it to be stolen. This step alone would begin to rebuild the shattered trust between the people and the state and ensure that the wealth of the nation is used for the nation, not a privileged few.

Breaking the Fever: Adopting a Counter-Cyclical Fiscal Policy

The second foundational repair is to break the feverish "boom-bust" cycle. Nigeria's habit of spending lavishly when oil prices are high and then crashing into austerity when they fall is a recipe for permanent instability. The solution is simple in concept but incredibly difficult in practice: save for a rainy day.

This requires a truly independent and well-managed Sovereign Wealth Fund (SWF), insulated from political pressure. While Nigeria has such a fund, its effectiveness has been limited by the constant political temptation to raid it. A successful SWF would have an iron-clad mandate to do three things. First, to stabilize the budget by saving excess revenue during booms and releasing it during busts, smoothing out the rollercoaster of government spending. Second, to invest in critical domestic infrastructure, like power and transport, that can help the non-oil economy grow. Third, to save for future generations, ensuring that when the oil eventually runs out, the country has a financial legacy to fall back on. This disciplined approach would end the economic chaos and create the predictability that long-term investors crave.

A Buffer for the Storm: A Flexible Exchange Rate

Finally, fixing the foundation means having the right shock absorbers. For years, the Central Bank of Nigeria has spent billions of dollars from its reserves to defend a specific value for the Naira. This creates a rigid system that breaks under pressure. A more flexible exchange rate regime would act as an automatic stabilizer. When oil prices fall, a flexible currency would naturally weaken. While this might sound bad, it has a powerful benefit: it instantly makes all other Nigerian products—from sesame seeds to leather goods—cheaper and more competitive on the global market. At the same time, it makes imports more expensive, encouraging Nigerians to buy locally produced goods. It helps the economy self-correct, insulating it from the worst of the oil price shocks.

Part 2: Building the New House - Forging a Diversified Future

With a more stable foundation, Nigeria can begin the real, long-term work of building a new economic structure. This is about nurturing the sectors that have been neglected for half a century and unleashing the immense potential of its people.

Powering the Dream: The Infrastructure Imperative

You cannot have an industrial revolution without power. In Nigeria, the lack of reliable electricity is the single greatest brake on economic growth. The entire nation generates less electricity than a single medium-sized American city.

Conclusion: Navigating the New Macroeconomic Reality

Our journey through the economic stories of 15 different nations paints a clear picture: the old maps no longer work. We are living in a world where the neat lines between different kinds of economic policy have dissolved, and the stable, predictable frameworks of the past have given way to something far more complex and uncertain. Looking at these countries together isn't just an academic exercise. It's like standing in a room with 15 windows, each looking out onto the same global storm but from a unique vantage point. What we see is a macroeconomic landscape in the middle of a radical transformation. The simple textbook theories are being rewritten in real-time by the messy, unpredictable realities of a new global era. The challenge for policymakers everywhere is navigating this new terrain without a reliable guide.

The ghost of the Zero Lower Bound (ZLB) still haunts the halls of the world's most powerful central banks. For years, the primary fear was an economic quicksand of deflation, where prices and growth get stuck in a downward spiral. Japan's multi-decade struggle is a sobering reminder of how incredibly difficult it is to escape this trap once it takes hold. Yet, in a stunningly fast pivot, the main challenge suddenly became the exact opposite. The U.S. Federal Reserve's whiplash-inducing shift from fighting too little inflation to battling too much of it shows how quickly the ground can shift. This legacy has normalized powerful but poorly understood tools like Quantitative Easing—essentially, injecting money directly into the financial system. But as the American experience demonstrates, nobody is quite sure how these tools truly work, making their future use a high-stakes gamble.

At the same time, the once-sacred wall separating monetary policy (the work of central banks) and fiscal policy (the work of governments) has crumbled. In fact, they have become entangled in a complicated, often clumsy, dance. In Japan, the policy of Yield Curve Control was a clear partnership, with the central bank actively helping the government keep its borrowing costs down. In Turkey, we saw a much darker version of this, where an unorthodox monetary policy essentially created a massive, hidden bill that the government would eventually have to pay, with catastrophic results. Meanwhile, in Germany, a decision to spend more at home sends powerful ripples across the entire Eurozone, influencing the monetary decisions for all its members. The lesson is undeniable: you can no longer judge one policy in isolation. The success or failure of economic management now depends entirely on the "policy mix" and how well the two partners can coordinate.

More than ever, we are forced to recognize that economics does not happen in a vacuum. It happens in the messy, passionate, and often irrational world of politics and people. The case of Turkey is a dramatic cautionary tale of what happens when political ambition overrules sound economic judgment, leading to an inflation crisis that devastated ordinary citizens. Argentina's painful cycle of debt and default shows how a lack of political unity can doom any chance of a stable, long-term economic plan. But politics can also be a force for positive change. Germany's historic decision to abandon decades of rigid fiscal ideology was a direct response to the immense pressure of geopolitical crisis. These stories prove that sound institutions and a basic level of social agreement aren't just helpful extras; they are the absolute foundation for effective economic stewardship.

Finally, the emerging markets of the world are performing a constant, high-stakes tightrope walk. They are forever trying to manage the "Impossible Trinity"—the difficult balancing act of controlling their currency's value, encouraging foreign investment, and setting their own economic course. Countries like India and Brazil have tried to build credibility by adopting formal inflation targets, essentially importing a rulebook from developed nations. However, that rulebook often clashes with the chaotic reality of managing a volatile currency and high public debt. For nations whose fortunes rise and fall with global commodity prices, like oil-rich Nigeria or resource-heavy Australia, life is a permanent rollercoaster. Their primary challenge is building effective shock absorbers—like a flexible exchange rate or a national savings fund—to soften the blows during the inevitable downturns.

Ultimately, this global tour reveals no magic formula or one-size-fits-all solution. Instead, it illuminates a set of timeless principles. It highlights the incredible value of credible, independent institutions that can act as a steady hand. It underscores the non-negotiable need for governments to manage their finances sustainably. It shows that the best policy frameworks are both disciplined and flexible, able to bend without breaking. Above all, it reminds us that every economic decision is made within a complex web of social and political forces. As leaders around the world navigate the uncertain terrain of the 21st-century economy, these lessons will be their most indispensable guide.

About Author

Azhar ul Haque Sario is a bestselling author and data scientist with a remarkable record of achievement. This Cambridge alumnus brings a wealth of knowledge to his work, holding an MBA, ACCA (Knowledge Level - FTMS College Malaysia and London College of Accountancy, London), BBA, and several Google certifications, including specializations in Google Data Analytics, Google Digital Marketing & E-commerce, and Google Project Management.

With ten years of business experience, Azhar combines practical expertise with his impressive academic background to craft insightful books. His prolific writing has resulted in an astounding 2810 published titles, earning him the record for the maximum Kindle editions and paperback books published by an individual author in one year, awarded by Asia Books of Records in 2024.

ORCID: https://orcid.org/0009-0004-8629-830X
Azhar.sario@hotmail.co.uk
https://www.linkedin.com/in/azharulhaquesario/

www.ingramcontent.com/pod-product-compliance
Lightning Source LLC
Chambersburg PA
CBHW031346230926
51848CB00002B/413
9783384730657